W9-BSR-755

A GUIDE TO THE
Art & Architecture
OF THE FRANCISCAN MONASTERY

AND COMMISSARIAT OF THE HOLY LAND
A National Historic Site

By Kirsten M. Jensen

with a Prefatory Note by Romano Stephen Almagno

Printed and bound in the United States of America

Library of Congress Control Number: 2007901798

ISBN: 1-885938-37-3 Paperback
ISBN: 1-885938-38-1 Hardcover

Published in 2007 by Cathedral Press
P.O. Box 777
Baltimore, Maryland 21203

Publisher: Daniel L. Medinger
Designer: Bernice Twum-Barimah Jones

Front cover photo by Brendan Cavanaugh
Back cover photo by Owen Sweeney III

Kirsten M. Jensen is also the author of the following books:

Picturing Arizona: The Photographic Record of the 1930s
Co-authored with Katherine G. Morrissey

Brendan Cavanaugh
Cloister Walk, designed by Murphy & Olmsted in partnership with John J. Earley.

TABLE OF
CONTENTS

PREFATORY NOTE

In the two years that I have had the holy privilege of living and working in this Monastery as Commissary and Guardian, two statements by the Catholic Church have continually surfaced in my mind and echoed in my heart. The first, from Vatican Council II's *Constitution on the Sacred Liturgy* (*Sacrosanctum Concilium*), published in 1963, states that "Ordinaries [that is: bishops] are to take care than in encouraging and favoring truly sacred art, they should seek for noble beauty rather than sumptuous display." The second, published thirty years later in 1992, appears in the *Catechism of the Catholic Church*:

Sacred art is true and beautiful when its form corresponds to its particular vocation: evoking and glorifying, in faith and adoration, the transcendent mystery of God… Genuine sacred art draws us to adoration, to prayer and to the love of God… For this reason bishops, personally or through delegates, should see to the promotion of sacred art, old and new, in all its forms…

Noble beauty…Sacred Art…Promotion of Sacred Art, old and new, in all its forms—these were the ideals and motives behind the dreams and work of Father Godfrey Schilling, OFM, Architect Aristides Leonori, and all who worked with them in the planning and building of this Monastery. We who live here, and those who come here, are the beneficiaries of their extraordinary accomplishments.

One hundred and eight years—February 1898 was the time when the first brick was laid, and September 1899 the time of the Monastery's dedication—are not, relatively speaking, very long ago. And yet, as the years pass and persons pass, and records grow yellow and brittle—so does the corporate memory of all that went into the planning and building of this glorious place. Thus, I asked Kirsten Jensen, my former student, and an art historian, to write the book that you now hold in your hands.

With gratitude to her and her scholarship—it is now with deep pride and great pleasure that I present to you her marvelous *Guide to the Art and Architecture* of this Franciscan Monastery, a place of noble beauty and sacred art, whose main purpose was, and remains to this day, to draw us "to adoration, to prayer and to the love of God"—which must, of course, be translated into active service with and for mankind.

Romano S. Almagno, OFM
Commissary and Guardian

The Franciscan Monastery from the south, ca. 1900.

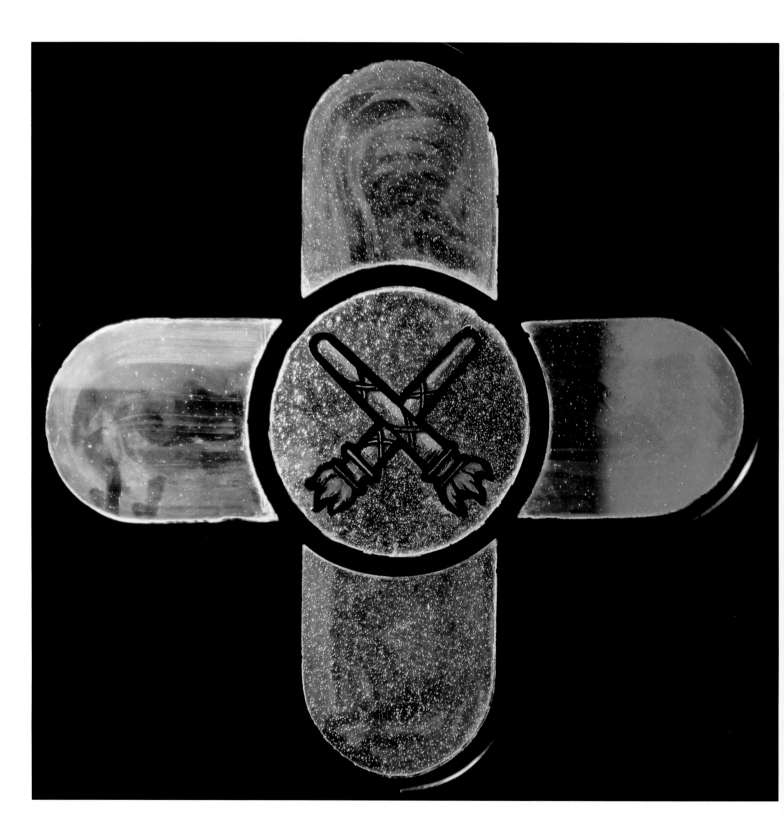

History of the Monastery and Commissariat of the Holy Land

T he Franciscan Monastery in Washington, D.C., was established to function as the United States' Commissariat of the Holy Land and also to raise awareness of the various shrines and sites in the Holy Land. The Franciscan Order has maintained a presence in the Holy Land for eight hundred years since 1219 when St. Francis left some of his disciples in Palestine as successors of the Crusaders and established there a Province of Order, which is still called the Custody of the Holy Land and is based in Jerusalem at the Church of the Holy Sepulcher. The Custody of the Holy Land comprises not only Israel and Jordan, but also Syria, Lebanon, Lower Egypt, and Cyprus. The Franciscans maintain numerous sanctuaries, parishes, mission churches, chapels, orphanages, colleges, and seminaries as well as secondary and elementary schools in these lands; in 1352, the Franciscans erected in Jerusalem the first public hospital, which continues to operate to this day. In addition to these institutions, the Custody has hospices for pilgrims and local people regardless of creed or nationality. The Custody is represented throughout the world by some seventy Commissariats, whose chief purpose is to raise awareness of the many shrines and sites in the Holy Land under the Custody's supervision, and to raise resources for their preservation and maintenance.

The Commissariat of the Holy Land in the United States was established in 1880 by Father Charles A. Vissani, OFM (1831-1896). Offices were at first temporarily located in a row of brownstones at 309 West 52nd Street, in New York City. In 1889, Vissani built the first Commissariat of the Holy Land forty blocks further north, at 143 West 95th Street.

First Commissariat of the Holy Land
in the United States, ca. 1890.

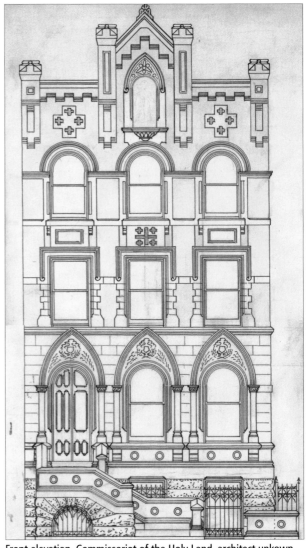

Front elevation, Commissariat of the Holy Land, architect unkown.

DESIGN INFLUENCE
The Victorian Gothic decoration chosen for the building's façade was typical of the period, but also reinforced the religious functions of the building.

The architect is unknown, but his drawings for the Commissariat have been preserved in the Monastery archives. The Victorian Gothic decoration chosen for the building's façade was typical of the period, but also reinforced the religious functions of the building. Vissani may have had his first thoughts about creating a larger Commissariat during the first organized American Catholic Pilgrimage to the Holy Land, organized by him in 1889. Unfortunately, Vissani was unable to realize this vision, as he died in 1896 in Nettuno, near Rome, where he had gone in the hope of recovering from an illness.

The fulfillment of Vissani's dream, the establishment of the present Monastery and Commissariat, was instead realized by Father Godfrey Schilling (1856-1934), who had become Commissary upon Vissani's death.

Father Godfrey Schilling and a companion
at the pyramids in Egypt, 1907.

Schilling and Italian architect Aristide Leonori originally planned to build a monastery on a high hill on Staten Island, New York, but Schilling became aware of available property in Brookland, on the outskirts of Washington, D.C. The appropriateness of relocating the Commissariat to the nation's capital, on a site not far from Catholic University, made the tract of land—complete with a high hill—extremely attractive. In 1897 Schilling purchased the 100-acre plot of land (which has decreased significantly in size over time) from the McCeeney family.

Originally, the land had been cultivated and prosperous, but by the time Schilling bought it, the old estate, which included a large clapboard house and several outbuildings, was in a desolate condition. The first six friars, known as the "pioneers," had to live in the ramshackle McCeeney house until the Monastery was completed two years later.

THE FIRST COMMISSARIAT

The Commissariat of the Holy Land in the United States was established in 1880 by Father Charles A. Vissani, OFM (1831-1896). Offices were at first temporarily located in a row of brownstones at 309 West 52nd Street, in New York City. In 1889, Vissani built the first Commissariat of the Holy Land forty blocks further north, at 143 West 95th Street.

The McCeeney House in 1897.

The first six friars, known as the "pioneers," had to live in the ramshackle McCeeney house ur the Monastery was completed two years later. Friar Isidore Germiat described the experien in a letter: "The place where the Monastery is located was a wilderness when we first came, surrounded by woods on all sides… There was an old house on the estate…where we spent part of the first winter, which w rather severe, eight below zero with heavy snowfalls."

Early friars and neighbors on the hilltop where the Monastery now stands.

One of the pioneers, Friar Isidore Germiat, described the e: perience in a letter:

> The place where the Monastery is located was a wilderness when we first came, surrounded by woods on all sides. The approach was a back road which comes up from what is today Taylor and 16th Streets NE. There was an old house on the estate…where we spent part of the first winter, which was rather severe—eight below zero with heavy snowfalls.

Germiat described the house as "made of rotten wood an filled with big rats," and several of the friars became ill durin the first winter.

While they were waiting for the Monastery to be completed the friars laid out walks, planted trees, and cultivated the fielc and a vegetable garden. In the meantime, Aristide Leono traveled to the Holy Land to measure shrines and sites tha Schilling intended to reproduce at the Monastery. Schillin meanwhile, raised money for construction by selling pape "building stones" for two cents each, or a dollar a row. Whe Leonori returned from his trip, work began in earnest.

Construction on the Memorial Church, ca. 1899.

Ground was broken early in February 1898 and the Monastery's cornerstone was laid on March 19. According to early guidebooks, the construction aroused intense interest, particularly as the outline of the Memorial Church, laid in the form of the five-fold Crusader's Cross, caused much speculation as to what the structure might look like and what it might house. The construction continued for a year and a half, until it was completed in late August 1899.

The Monastery and its Memorial Church were dedicated on the feast of the Stigmata of St. Francis, September 17, 1899. A multitude of religious and secular dignitaries, including Cardinal Gibbons, Bishop Blenk of Puerto Rico and later the archbishop of New Orleans, and the president of Georgetown University, attended, and according to reports at the time, more than ten thousand pilgrims came to witness the ceremony. The dedication ceremony was reported in a lengthy feature article in the *Washington Post* on September 18:

Superb reproductions of the Stables at Bethlehem, the Home of the Holy Family at Nazareth, and the Holy Sepulcher, altars, and monuments, which lend inspiration to the student, all are to be found in the monastery. The foremost ecclesiastical architect of Rome, Senor Aristides Leonori, has given to them his best efforts. For the purpose of making them exact facsimiles he visited Bethlehem, Nazareth, and other sacred spots, taking measurements and keeping in mind the character of the stone and structure. Those who saw his handiwork yesterday are satisfied that he made a most faithful counterpart.

The completed Memorial Church at the time of its dedication, September 1899.

As an 1899 photograph of the Monastery demonstrates, the surrounding area, now known as Brookland, was much different one hundred years ago than it is today.

Pilgrims to the Monastery had to use dirt roads that were frequently muddy, and rutted from wagons and, later, cars. In 1919, the friars petitioned for an extension of the electric trolley line—the forerunner of today's Metro and bus systems—to provide better transportation for pilgrims arriving from Union Station. By the 1920s, Quincy Avenue had been paved; but the friars' petition to Congress for further pavement was only successful after they agreed to cede portions of the property for new roads. The 1920s through the 1930s was a great period of pilgrimage, and the pope granted indulgences to many of the shrines, so that those who could not travel to the Holy Land could have spiritual benefits similar to pilgrims who traveled to the Holy Land itself.

A LONG ROAD
Although the Monastery and Memorial Church were finished in 1899, only a portion of Schilling's vision had been realized. Leonori and other Italian architects had made meticulous drawings and measurements of many more sites and shrines, and it would take nearly thirty more years before the Monastery was complete.

Dedication of the Monastery and its Memorial Church, September 17, 1899.

A view of the Monastery grounds and Brookland, ca. 1903.

Buses for pilgrims, parked along 14th Street, ca. 1930.

Initially, the Monastery included a seminary to prepare friars for service in the Holy Land. The seminary no longer exists, but the Monastery still prepares some friars for the same purpose and receives friars who come to Washington to study at Catholic University or other institutions in the area.

Although the Monastery and Memorial Church were finished in 1899, only a portion of Schilling's vision had been realized. Leonori and other Italian architects had made meticulous drawings and measurements of many more sites and shrines, and it would take nearly thirty more years before the Monastery was complete. The shrines and grottos in the lower gardens were constructed between 1903-1926, the Rosary Portico that encloses the Monastery and its upper gardens was completed in 1927, St. Francis Hall was completed in 1932, and the wing containing the visitor lobby and Monastery offices was constructed in 1941. Additionally, renovations to the interior of Memorial Church were undertaken during the 1920s and again in 1949-1953 as the Monastery celebrated its fiftieth anniversary, or golden jubilee. Throughout the 1950s and into the 1970s, more shrines, sculptures, and mosaics were added to the lower gardens, and the gardens themselves developed from basic tree and shrub planting to the beautiful floral landscaping seen today nearly year-round.

This guidebook is intended to provide a thorough history of the Monastery, Memorial Church, and the gardens from 1899 to the present. Numerous known and unknown artists, artisans, and craftspeople have contributed to the creation of the Monastery, which was designated a National Historic Site in 1994. Their contributions are described here to the best of our ability and extent of our knowledge, with research grounded in the Monastery's archival and photograph collections, which are available for research in Special Collections at the Catholic University of America Library.

The guide is written from an art historical perspective, rather than a purely religious one, and it is intended for the enjoyment of visitors of all religions and creeds.

Artists and
ARCHITECTS

T hroughout the Monastery's more than one hundred year history, visitors have enjoyed the work of a number of leading artists and architects who were instrumental in its design and construction. Many of the individuals who designed and constructed the Basilica of the National Shrine of the Immaculate Conception, only one mile away, were involved in sculptural and architectural work at the Monastery. Murphy & Olmsted, the architectural firm that designed buildings for the Monastery during the 1920s and 1930s, was responsible for many of the buildings at Catholic University of America and also assisted in the design and construction of the National Shrine. John Joseph Earley, who created the main altar for the National Shrine, worked extensively at the Monastery beginning in 1909. A number of artists also contributed to the decoration of the Monastery Church, including painters Charles Svendsen and Charles Bosseron Chambers, and sculptor and mosaic artist Frederick C. Shrady. These individuals, as well as others who remain anonymous or about whom little is known, helped to make the Monastery the unique site that it is today.

ARCHITECTS

Aristide Leonori (1857-1928). Engineer and architect Aristide Leonori was born in Rome on July 28, 1856, to Raffaele and Anna Ianari. His early education was entrusted to a priest, and when he was eight, Leonori entered Collegio Romano in Rome. In 1880 he graduated with a degree as an architectural engineer. While in Rome, Leonori designed at least five churches and several hospitals, including St. Patrick's, the Irish National Church in Rome, which was completed in 1892, and Santa Croce on the via Flamina in 1912. One of Leonori's biggest projects was the design and construction of the Church of St. Joseph in Cairo, Egypt, built in 1909 with the assistance of Father Godfrey Schilling.

ARISTIDE LEONORI
One of Leonori's biggest projects was the design and construction of the Church of St. Joseph in Cairo, Egypt, built in 1909 with the assistance of Father Godfrey Schilling.

Aristide Leonori (left) and Father Godfrey Schilling in the Monastery garden, ca. 1907-1909.

MURPHY & OLMSTED ARCHITECTURAL FIRM

Murphy & Olmsted created the master plan for Catholic University and designed a number of the buildings on its campus in the Collegiate Gothic style, including John K. Mullen Library, Curley Hall, and the School of Music.

Leonori and Father Godfrey supervising the construction of St. Joseph's in Cairo, Egypt, in 1909.

Leonori's work in Washington eventually led to several other significant commissions in the United States, including the Cathedral Basilica of St. Louis (1907); St. Joseph's Cathedral in Buffalo, NY (1912), and Holy Rosary Church in Washington, D.C. (1923).

Murphy & Olmsted. The architectural firm Murphy & Olmsted was formed in 1911 by architects Frederick Vernon Murphy (1879-1959) and Walter B. Olmsted (d. 1936), who had worked together as draftsmen in the Capital Architect's Office. Frederick Murphy was born in Fond du Lac, Wisconsin. In 1882, his father died in a train accident, and Murphy moved with his mother and sister to Chicago where he later attended the Art Institute of Chicago. At the age of twenty, Murphy moved to Washington, D.C., for a position as a draftsman in the Capital's Supervising Architect's Office, and in 1905, he received a scholarship from the Washington Architectural Club to study abroad. Between 1905 and 1909 he attended the École des Beaux-Arts in Paris—then the world's pre-eminent school for architecture; he earned his diploma in 1915. Among his classmates at the École was Charles Van Allen, who would later design the Chrysler Building. Little is known about Walter B. Olmsted, who is not related to the landscape architect Frederick Law Olmsted.

In 1911, Murphy established the School of Architecture at Catholic University of America, where he taught architecture in the Beaux-Arts tradition. Murphy & Olmsted created the master plan for Catholic University and designed a number of the buildings on its campus in the Collegiate Gothic style, including John K. Mullen Library, Curley Hall, and the School of Music. At the Monastery, Murphy & Olmsted designed the Rosary Portico and Pilgrimage Hall and were partners with John Earley in the design and construction of the Portiuncula Chapel, the Chapel of St. Anne, and the Ascension Chapel located in the Monastery's gardens.

James Earley, John Joseph Earley & Earley Studio. James Earley (d. 1909) was an Irish immigrant who worked as a stonecutter in New York before moving to Washington, D.C., where he designed, among other things, the Buffalo Nickel for the United States Mint. In Foggy Bottom James Earley established a studio and stonecutting workshop that executed a number of sculptures for the Monastery, including the bas-reliefs for three of the chapels in Memorial Church. His son, John Joseph Earley (1881-1945), was an artist, an architect, and above all, a master of concrete. In addition to Aristide Leonori, the Earleys—particularly John—were the most influential in shaping the look of the Monastery and the grounds as we see them today. John Earley took over his father's studio in 1906, and, working in conjunction with a business partner and mentor, Basil Gordon Taylor, gradually transformed the studio into a thriving business with projects in Washington and throughout the United States.

The Earley Studio was extremely active in the Washington, D.C., area. Between 1912 and 1936, John Earley constructed the walls, stairs, and balustrades of Meridian Hill Park. The aggregate employed in the polychromed concrete that he used included earth-toned stones dredged from the Potomac River. He also constructed the nave and aisles of the Shrine of the Sacred Heart, completed in 1923, work which was highlighted in the publication, *Substance, Form, and Color Through Concrete*, published by the Portland Cement Company. For this project, he expanded his palette to include glass, ceramics, and other stones, providing the foundation for the work he would later undertake at the Monastery. Earley was also responsible for panels at the Walker Building on 15th Street NW, ceilings for the Justice Department, ceilings and walkways at Dulles Airport, and the five Polychrome Houses in Silver Spring. In Chicago, he worked with Lorado Taft on the Fountain of Time (1922) in Hyde Park, and in Wilmette, Illinois, his Bahai' Temple, completed posthumously in 1953, still sparkles in the sun.

Although Earley's artistic grounding lay in the medieval crafts guild tradition, he chose for his life work the very modern medium of concrete. Technical innovation was his passion and he was always seeking better ways to build beautiful, modern structures. In the 1930s, Earley and the Earley Studio helped the Federal Bureau of Standards find ways to enhance the strength and durability of stucco and concrete; Earley also patented a number of production methods and processes. He is best known, however, for the invention of the so-called Earley Process, an innovation that he called variously "architectural," "polychrome," or "mosaic" concrete. Traditional concrete involves mixing small stones, or aggregate, with cement and water to form the body of the concrete. The Earley Process employed colored stones as the aggregate, which was then exposed by scraping away a layer of cement with wire brushes.

In developing the Earley Process, John Earley was strongly influenced by the color theories of Michel Chevreul and Ogden N. Rood, the same theories that underlay the techniques of the painters associated with the Impressionist and Pointillist painting styles. These color theories showed that when contrasting colors (red, yellow, blue) are placed next to each other, they blend optically to form hues of even values. Earley believed that the clarity of color and surface texture found in Impressionist and Pointillist paintings could also be found in concrete. He later observed that, "by considering the particles of aggregate as spots of color in juxtaposition, all the knowledge and much of the technique of the Impressionist or the Pointillist school of painting, was immediately applicable to concrete…"

At the Monastery, the work of James and John Earley as well as other artists working for Earley Studio is extensive. In addition to the reliefs behind the altars in three of the four chapels in the Memorial Church, James Earley also designed the rosettes and stuccowork employed throughout the church and its dome. After his father's death, John Earley continued his association with the Monastery, designing the bas-relief panels in the apse and nave of Memorial Church as well as many of the altars. The construction of the catacombs was also overseen by Earley, as was the Rosary Portico, the statue of St. Christopher, and much of the work on the Grottos and shrines in the gardens.

THE EARLEY INFLUENCE
At the Monastery, the work of James and John Earley as well as other artists working for Earley Studio is extensive. In addition to the reliefs behind the altars in three of the four chapels in the Memorial Church, James Earley also designed the rosettes and stuccowork employed throughout the church and its dome.
The construction of the Catacombs was also overseen by Earley, as was the Rosary Portico, the statue of St. Christopher, and much of the work on the Grottos and shrines in the gardens.

Earley Studio artisans scrape away the aggregate on the statue of St. Christopher, ca. 1926.

Friar Baumann and the Office of Franciscan Art and Architecture. Friar Cajetan Baumann (d. 1969), OFM, FAIA, directed the Office of Franciscan Art and Architecture in New York from its establishment in 1946 until 1969. The office provided architectural and design services to Franciscan Provinces in North America as well as to diocesan authorities in other religious communities. Although it was not engaged in general practice, the Office of Franciscan Art and Architecture attracted a number of secular architects and designers who later earned national reputations: Paul Damaz (b. 1917), the office's chief designer, who helped design the United Nations building in New York and received the Arnold Brunner Award in 1958; and Gottfried Bohm (b. 1920), who received the coveted Pritzker Prize—architecture's highest honor—in 1986. Some of the projects the office completed under Friar Baumann's direction are the chapel and friary at St. Bonaventure University in New York, and the House of Theology in Centerville, Ohio. Friar Baumann's designs were incredibly progressive, providing modern interpretations of Gothic architecture. Under the direction of Friar Baumann, the Office of Franciscan Art and Architecture began work on renovation of the interior of the Monastery Church in 1950.

Friar Baumann earned his bachelor's (1941) and master's (1945) degrees in architecture from Columbia University, where he later served on the Board of Governors of the School of Architecture; he became a licensed architect in New York State in 1945. Friar Baumann was active in the National Committee on Religious Buildings, the Architectural League of New York, the National Sculpture Society, the New York Building Congress, and the National Council of Architectural Registration Boards. Friar Baumann was also the American representative to the International Commission for the Restoration of the Basilica of the Holy Sepulcher in Jerusalem.

ARTISTS

Charles C. Svendsen (1871-1959). Charles Svendsen was born in Cincinnati, Ohio, and was the son of J.F. Svendsen, an entrepreneur who had established a banner, flag, and military equipment business there in 1866. Svendsen studied at the Cincinnati Art Academy with artist Thomas Noble and later in Paris with the French academic painter William Adolphe Bouguereau at the Academy Julian, and at the Academy Colarossi with Gabriel Ferrier. In 1898, Svendsen left Paris for a tour of Egypt. He returned to the United States with numerous sketches, drawings, and paintings, which later influenced his work. Svendsen specialized in religious and historical paintings, and in addition to the paintings he made for the Monastery, his work can be seen in Cincinnati's St. Xavier's Church and Mt. St. Mary's Seminary in Norwood, Ohio. Svendsen also painted panels for the Cathedral of Dacca, India, and St. Joseph Church in Nazareth, Palestine. For the Monastery, Svendsen painted panels in the Martyrs' and Annunciation Crypts, the catacombs, and the Bethlehem Grotto. His painting *Youth in the Temple* is located beneath the Sacred Heart Altar and above the entrance to the Bethlehem Grotto.

Charles Bosseron Chambers (1882-1964). Artist Charles Bosseron Chambers was known for his figurative work, mainly portraits or works with religious themes. Chambers was born in St. Louis; his father was an Irish captain in the British Army and his mother was a member of an established French family in St. Louis. According to his niece, Chambers later adopted the middle name "Bosseron" because he felt his last name "too plain" to reflect his French heritage.

Like many American artists at the turn of the century, Chambers studied abroad, first at the Berlin Royal Academy, where he spent six years studying with Louis Schultz. Later he studied with Alois Hrdliczka at the Royal Academy in Vienna and with Johannes Schumacher in Dresden. In 1916, Chambers returned to the United States and settled into a studio at the Carnegie Studios in New York City. It was there that he painted *Light of the World*, the most popular religious painting at the time. Chambers later illustrated Scribner Classics' version of Sir Walter Scott's *Quentin Durward*. For the Monastery, Chambers painted a number of works, the best known of which were his cover illustrations for the Commissariat's publication, *Crusader's Almanac*.

Frederick S. Shrady (1907-1990). Although he had no formal training as a sculptor Frederick C. Shrady grew up in an environment in which art—particularly sculpture–was paramount. Shrady's father was the sculptor Henry Merwin Shrady (1871-1922), who created the Grant Memorial in Washington, D.C., and is well known for his sculptures of Native Americans and the wildlife of the West. Shrady graduated from Oxford University in England in 1931 and then moved to the Montparnasse district in Paris, where he was surrounded by the heady artistic milieu of Picasso, Leger, and Andre Derain, who was a mentor and friend. It was during his nine years in Paris that Shrady began to paint, an artistic medium he gave up following World War II, deciding to pursue sculpture instead. During the war, Shrady worked as an interpreter for the U.S. Army's Fine Arts and Monuments Department. His first work as a sculptor was a portrait head of Father Martin D'Arcy, SJ, now in the collection of the Metropolitan Museum of Art in New York. Among his other works are *Joan of Arc* for the St. Paul Cathedral in Pittsburgh, Pennsylvania; *Peter, Fisher of Men* (1969), in the plaza of Fordham University's Lincoln Center Campus; *Mother Seton* (1975) in St. Patrick's Cathedral, New York; and *Fatima* (1982), in the Vatican Gardens. At the Monastery, Shrady designed a number of mosaics and also sculpted the statue of Father Godfrey Shilling situated on the piazza in the upper gardens.

Murphy & Olmsted, *Monastery Dome and Cupola*
Showing the proper silhouette, ca. 1920.

THE MEMORIAL CHURCH

T he Memorial Church of the Holy Sepulcher was designed by Italian architect Aristide Leonori in 1897. Unlike the shrines that are located throughout the church and its grounds, Memorial Church was not intended to be a replica of any extant structure, rather it is intended to call to mind existing structures in the Holy Land and Italy—hence the name, Memorial Church. The Memorial Church is a mixture of various architectural styles that reflect the Monastery's connection to the ancient sites and traditions associated with the Holy Land and Italy, as well as architectural styles that were popular during its construction and later renovations.

The floor plan of the church is the five-fold Crusader Cross of Jerusalem, and it is designed in the Byzantine style after Hagia Sophia in Constantinople.

Interior of the Memorial Church, ca. 1900, showing the Altar of Calvary and the Lady Chapel.

Leonori combined the Byzantine church plan with Italian Romanesque elements on the exterior and Italian Renaissance architecture on the interior. Leonori's sunken dome required a creative solution in order to provide the filtered natural light essential to both Romanesque and Byzantine church designs. In traditional Byzantine designs, the dome would have been placed on top of a row of windows, or a clerestory, that would have allowed natural light to enter the church. Leonori's solution came in the form of an oculus at the top of the dome, which allows natural light to filter into the interior, illuminating the main altar below. For building material, Leonori chose bricks in a warm yellow tone, a simple yet beautiful skin that allowed the church to harmonize with the landscape, but also turned it into a glowing beacon at sunset.

The exterior of the church has remained largely unchanged since 1899. In 1918, architects Murphy & Olmsted, who were then working on the design for the Rosary Portico, presented the Monastery with new designs for the front entrance,

DESIGN INFLUENCES
The floor plan of the church is the five-fold Crusader Cross of Jerusalem, and it is designed in the Byzantine style after Hagia Sophia in Constantinople. Leonori combined the Byzantine church plan with Italian Romanesque elements on the exterior and Italian Renaissance architecture on the interior.

Interior of the Memorial Church.

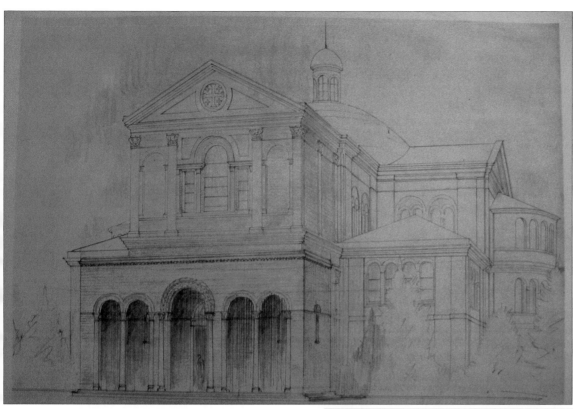

Murphy & Olmsted, *Front Elevation, the Memorial Church*, ca. 1920.

Hamilton & Wilson, *Plan for Renovations to the Memorial Church and Friary*, ca. 1940-1941.

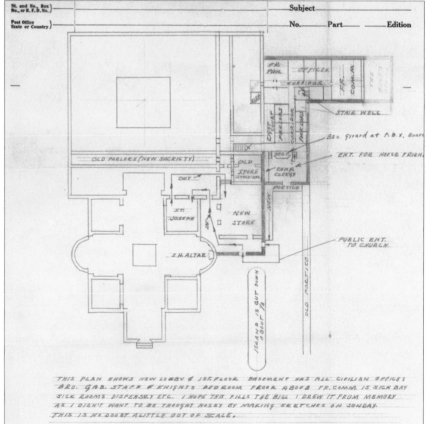

which would have provided a stronger and more cohesive appearance to the overall façade as well as a seamless transition between the Portico and the church. However, the design was not adopted, and the façade was first changed in 1941, when a new wing was added in front of the friary. The addition was intended to provide better accommodation for the pilgrims visiting the church and shrines, a gift shop, offices, and an infirmary for the friars. Murphy & Olmsted sketched an early articulation of how the new vestibule might be achieved, but it was architect Hamilton Wilson who provided the plan that was adopted and completed in 1942.

Frederick Shrady, *I am the Resurrection and the Life*, mosaic, 1949, entrance to the Memorial Church.

Frederick Shrady, *Deus Meus et Omina*, mosaic, 1949, entrance to the Blessed Sacrament Chapel.

In 1949, the mosaic now seen above the main entrance to Memorial Church replaced a bas-relief by James Earley that had deteriorated. The mosaic was designed and executed by Frederick C. Shrady of Ridgefield, Connecticut, who also designed the mosaics that decorate the entrance to the Blessed Sacrament Chapel and the church's vestibules.

Mosaics designed by Frederick Shrady in 1949 to decorate the exterior of the church vestibules.

Interior of the Memorial Church, ca. 1898, showing the Altar of Calvary and men laying the terrazzo floor.

The interior of Memorial Church has been renovated and re-envisioned several times over the past one hundred years. Photographs of the interior from 1899 reveal an austere church, painted in soft grey with white trim to replicate the marble molding and wainscoting characteristic of churches built during the Renaissance. The barrel vaults, ceiling, and dome were decorated with plaster rosettes, also painted white, and the floor was Italian terrazzo marble with tiles laid in the pattern of the Jerusalem Cross. At the center of the cross beneath the dome was the main marble altar over which was placed a white baldachino, designed in an Italian Renaissance style but constructed of wood and painted white to resemble marble. Natural light streamed in through clear windowpanes, brightening an interior that initially did not have artificial light.

The overall effect of the whole design was one of lightness—the barrel vaults and dome seem to soar above the smooth and sparkling marble floor; chairs were only used in the church for special occasions.

Over the years the austere Renaissance interior began to change as shrines, altars, and windows were added. These changes began in 1906, when the Lady Chapel was completed, and continued through the 1920s with the additions of the three other chapels and the relief sculptures to the four altars in the apses and nave. In 1931, most of the stained-glass windows, designed by the Royal Bavarian Art Institute in Munich, Germany, were installed.

THE ALTARS

The Memorial Church has four altars, located in the nave, apse, and transepts of the church: the Altar of Calvary, the Altar of the Holy Ghost, the Altar of the Sacred Heart, and the Altar of Tabor. Behind each altar is a series of polychromed, life-size, high bas-relief panels depicting significant moments from the life of Christ and St. Francis. Originally, the four altars stood alone and with very little decoration, as seen in this photograph from about 1900.

The Altar of Transfiguration was installed in 1916, and the relief panel was one of the first commissions for John Earley, marking a continuation of the work at the Monastery begun by his father, James. The other altars were replaced between 1923-1925, when Earley was commissioned to design new ones as well as relief panels to line the walls behind them.

Earley had originally intended for the relief sculptures to remain unpainted so that they would be reminiscent of the sculptures of Bernini and Maderno, two leading sculptors of the Renaissance. The superiors of the Monastery community at the time, however, wanted them to be colored and also requested that each panel include a painted background to situate more clearly for the viewer the moment it depicted. It is likely that the sculptural panels in the four chapels were similarly painted at this time, as they had not been painted

Murphy & Olmsted, *Design for the Stations of the Cross*, ca. 1933.

upon installation nearly twenty years earlier. Earley also objected to the use of artificial spotlights to cast light on the relief panels, preferring instead the natural light that would filter through the stained-glass windows throughout the Church. Earley argued that the use of natural light would more correctly replicate the light in earlier Romanesque and Byzantine churches on which Memorial Church was based.

Critics apparently agreed with Earley's assessment on both accounts. Writing for the *Washington Post* in 1931, Sibilla Skidelsky remarked that, "without these features, Mr. Earley's [reliefs] would have been a magnificent piece of art." The friars, however, did not necessarily want high art, but rather art that would appeal to the emotions and senses of visitors making a pilgrimage to the Monastery. Painted or not, eighty years after their creation and installation, Earley's reliefs remain one of the most popular features of the Memorial Church.

STATIONS OF THE CROSS

The Stations of the Cross are located throughout the Memorial Church. The Stations that we see today were not the first to be installed in the church. The original Stations, of which there remains no record, were considered "too modest" by the late 1920s. Following the installation of the new altars in 1927, the Monastery began a lengthy process of visualizing a design for new Stations that would not only be in keeping with the church's overall Byzantine architectural style, but which also reflected the increasing importance of shrines and altars in Memorial Church at Mt. St. Sepulcher. The process of designing new Stations involved numerous artists, sculptors, architects, and companies, and reveals how the friars attempted to shape the look of Memorial Church as well as the visitors' experience of it.

The Monastery first contacted Emil Frei Jr., who at that time was supervising the installation of the church's stained-glass windows. In a letter from June 1930, now in the Monastery's archives, Frei mentions that he is sending samples of Stations from the company's studio in St. Louis, which managed all mosaic work. These Stations, Frei noted, were similar to ones the company was preparing for a church in Seattle, and would assist the Monastery in visualizing the final effect of the Stations installed in the Memorial Church. The designs were not well received by the friars, and in 1931, another letter from Frei indicates that his studio artists were working on revised designs for the Stations.

Matters were apparently not resolved with Emil Frei Studio, and in 1933, the Monastery contacted D'Ascenso Studios in Philadelphia to submit designs for the Stations. Over the next year, D'Ascenso sent a number of sample mosaics and frame designs that could be used as starting points for conceptualizing the Monastery's own versions. Nicola D'Ascenso wrote in November 1934 about one design, "Personally, I think that the effect is very fine indeed with the frame suggested by the architects, and I hope that this meets with your approval." He was sorely disappointed when he received the reply that, while the Monastery found the design to be quite beautiful, the effect was lost because once installed the colors of the proposed mosaic were too dark. D'Ascenso subsequently lightened the background colors and darkened the shading surrounding the figures, but this, too, proved unsatisfactory. Another plan was submitted, which the friars deemed too expensive, even after the studio suggested ways in which the design could be modified to reduce the overall cost.

In February 1935, Friar Anthony of the Monastery wrote to D'Ascenso: "We feel we must tell you that the chances are decidedly against placing this order with you, due to the cost of your type of station…We hardly need tell you of our regret at being forced by conditions not within our control, to arrive at this decision." Friar Anthony noted, however, that the Monastery would hold onto the samples recently supplied by D'Ascenso just in case the company decided to negotiate further. D'Ascenso did. In a letter to Friar Anthony in March, in which one can hear the sound of his heart breaking, D'Ascenso made an offer to reduce the number of figures in the mosaic and eliminate the raised China gold in the halos, as well as all decorative backgrounds. "To have gone so far with you in this matter," he wrote, "and to lose it now would indeed be most disappointing, and I sincerely hope that you will be able to see your way clear to spend the required amount for a good thing, artistically and structurally, for your Monastery Chapel." The final design incorporated frames made by the Monastery's architects Murphy & Olmsted, who had been contracted to develop the architectural support for the Stations as early as 1933.

STATIONS OF THE CROSS
The process of designing new Stations involved numerous artists, sculptors, architects, and companies, and reveals how the friars attempted to shape the look of Memorial Church as well as the visitors' experience of it.

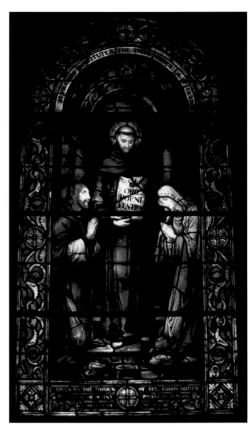

Royal Bavarian Art Institute, *Christ Among the Doctors, The Sacred Heart,* and *The Institution of the Third Order.*

All of D'Ascenso's efforts came to naught, and by July, the studio's account with the monastery was considered closed—but not entirely. In January 1938 an insurance broker contacted the Monastery seeking the whereabouts of a few of the samples and designs the studio had sent to the Monastery. After much correspondence back and forth, Friar Anthony returned the designs to Philadelphia, requesting that D'Ascenso not use the designs for the frame, drawn over the Station design by Murphy & Olmsted, as they were copyrighted. By May 1938, all communication between D'Ascenso and the Monastery had ceased.

In the end, the Stations of the Cross were designed by Benziger Brothers of New York, a now-defunct firm that had a long history in Europe—dating to the 18th century—of designing church decorations and religious art objects. While the story of the design of the Stations of the Cross for Memorial Church has a whiff of controversy, the ending is a happy one for those who visit the Monastery. Installed in 1939, the Benziger Stations we see today are a simplified version of the designs submitted by D'Ascenso Studio in 1935, with modifications to the original frame design by Murphy & Olmsted. The decision to have the figures in relief rather than mosaic was likely made to maintain consistency with

Royal Bavarian Art Institute, *Christ Giving the Keys to St. Peter, The Agony in the Garden,* and *The Resurrection.*

the other relief panels in the church. The fourteen Stations are sculpted polychrome alabaster on a ground of variegated silver mosaic, and the frames are carved in marble from Botticino, Italy, and inlaid with gold mosaic and olive wood. Funds for the Stations were donated by the Knights of Mt. St. Sepulcher.

THE SACRISTY

The Sacristy, where the friars store vestments and vessels used for Mass, is situated inside the Monastery Cloister, or friary, and is not accessible to the public. Around 1930, the old Sacristy was remodeled into the present tour lobby, and a new Sacristy was created from two existing parlors in the friary. These parlors had direct access to the friary's courtyard, and it was decided that great advantage could be made of this natural light source with stained-glass windows. Six windows were ordered from the Royal Bavarian Art Institute in Munich, Germany, and installed in 1931. These windows are: *Christ among the Doctors, The Sacred Heart, The Institution of the Third Order, Christ Giving the Keys to St. Peter, The Resurrection,* and *The Agony in the Garden.*

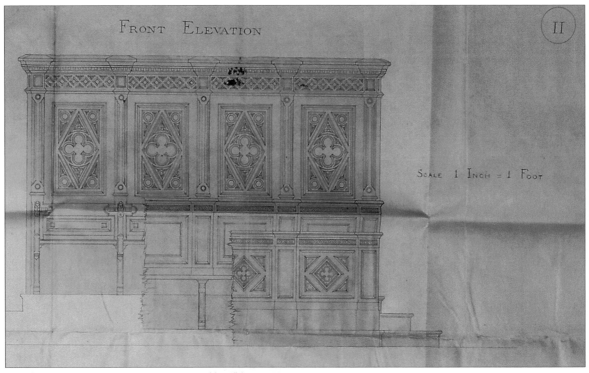

Aristide Leonori, *Front Elevation, Choir Loft* (detail), ca. 1898.

The design for *Christ among the Doctors* is based upon a painting by German artist Heinrich Hofmann (1824-1911), *Christ in the Temple* (1886), which John D. Rockefeller donated to Riverside Church in New York City. The friars and Emil Frei, who was acting as liaison between the Monastery and the artists in Munich, had a lengthy discussion concerning the design of this window. Frei believed that the window's inscription taken from the Gospel of Luke, "They found Him in the Temple," did not correspond to Hoffman's painting, which does not include Jesus' parents. To solve the dilemma and make the image correspond to the text, the artists in Munich inserted the figures of Mary and Joseph behind Jesus and the scholars. Initially, the friars were not pleased with the addition, but they must have been persuaded by Frei's reasoning, as the window installed in the Sacristy contains the figures of Mary and Joseph.

NORTH CHOIR AND ORGAN LOFT

Like the Sacristy, both the North Choir and the Organ Loft are not accessible to the public, but both contain architectural details, including stained-glass windows from the Royal Bavarian Art Institute in Munich, that are significant to the overall decorative program first envisioned by the Monastery's architect, Aristide Leonori. The North Choir functions as the private chapel for the friars, and although Memorial Church and the Cloister are designed in a Romanesque-Byzantine style, Leonori chose to design the North Choir in a Gothic style.

Royal Bavarian Art Institute, *Assumption of the Virgin* (original conception).

Assumption of the Virgin as installed in the Choir Loft.

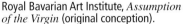

The North Choir is decorated with a number of stained-glass windows, including three of the Crusader Windows that decorate the Altar of Transfiguration. Other windows include a depiction of Christ appearing at Emmaus and the Immaculate Conception based on the Baroque Spanish artist Murillo's painting of the same subject. The original design submitted by the artists in Munich showed the Virgin surrounded by rays of light and framed by a trefoil arch.

Royal Bavarian Art Institute, *Supper at Emmaus* (left), *St. Bonaventure* (right).

However, the friars, stating that the "use of the Gothic or pointed nimbus on these windows strikes a decidedly discordant note," preferred a significantly modified design that eliminated the architectural elements and minimized the rays emanating from behind the Virgin. So, the window that was installed in 1931 depicted the Virgin surrounded by Putti (cherubs) with two angels kneeling at her feet.

Royal Bavarian Art Institute, *St. Nicolas Tavelic* (right) and *St. Charles Borromeo* (left).

Just outside the door leading into the North Choir from the Cloister is another window with a full-length portrait of St. Bonaventure (1221-1274), who was saved from death in childhood by the intercession of St. Francis. Bonaventure entered the Order of Friars Minor in Paris in 1243 and became one of the most revered professors, writers, and ministers of the Franciscan Order, as well as the order's first cardinal.

Although it is accessible only through the Cloister, the Organ Loft, which is located above the Chapel of St. Francis, can be seen from Memorial Church. On a sunny day, visitors can see the four stained-glass windows installed along the eastern wall of Memorial Church. These windows commemorate, from left to right: St. Nicolas Tavelic, OFM; St. Charles Borromeo, Third Order; St. Bede the Venerable; and St. Didacus, OFM.

GOLDEN JUBILEE RENOVATIONS

By the late 1930s, potted plants covered the marble steps of the main altar, and the cross design in the terrazzo floor had become obscured by carpeting placed to protect it from further deterioration. The paint on the walls, vaults and dome had begun to peel, the natural light filtering through the stained-glass windows was less effective as a light source, and the once glorious space seemed dark, crowded, and out-of-date. By the late 1940s, the Memorial Church was definitely in need of renovation. In 1948, Friar Baumann was hired to help the friars restore and redesign Memorial Church for its jubilee and to meet the needs of the next fifty years. Under Friar Baumann's direction, the once Romanesque and Italian Renaissance interior of the church was brought into stylistic harmony with its exterior design. The once-beautiful terrazzo floor was taken up and replaced with marble; the wooden entrance doors were replaced with others made of bronze; the main altar was rebuilt with a new and lower predella and its marble baldachino was replaced with a new one of bronze; the stained-glass windows were cleaned and repaired; and the entire interior was redecorated and repainted; the shrines, altars, and areas of the Catacombs were restored and renovated.

Friar Baumann and Rambusch Brothers, *New color scheme for the Memorial Church*, ca. 1949

The most extensive of the renovations was the redesign of the interior concept of Memorial Church, which involved much more than surface painting. Friar Baumann worked with Rambusch Company of New York to create a decorative scheme in which tonalities and notes of color were used to increase the unity and effectiveness of Memorial Church's interior. The design scheme chosen was a background color of soft beige, which lightens towards the ceiling vaults and dome, with muted accents in terra cotta, reds, greens, and lapis lazuli, with each chapel painted in a scheme based on a different dominant color.

Equally extensive was the new plan to illuminate the church, and to integrate the lighting plan to harmonize with the new colors of the interior. New lights were installed in the ceiling, and eight bronze hanging fixtures were installed so that illumination was increased by light reflecting off their polished surfaces. The resulting effect makes the interior seem illuminated without revealing the light source, and conveys the impression of restrained dignity shot through with ordered spots of color. As one moves through the church from apse to nave, from the main altar to the chapels, the effect of light and color shifts, creating different experiences of the space. The colors of the new marble floor, redesigned with tiles of soft tan and grey punctuated with spots of color, provide a base for the overall design, above which soar the vaults of white and gold, with the subdued glow of filtered light through the stained-glass windows that changes according to the time of day and season. In each aisle bright mosaics lead from the four ends of the church to the main altar, and the floors of the corner chapels blend in tone with the main floor, but the different pattern employed for each chapel distinguishes them as separate spaces in the church.

Friar Baumann and Rambusch Brothers, *Color Scheme for the Altar of Tabor,* ca. 1949.

Rambusch Brothers, two design concepts for the new Main Altar.

The whole scheme was conceived to lead the eye to the altar, the main focus of the church and the climax of the new decorative scheme. The original marble baldachino was dismantled and replaced with a striking bronze baldachino designed by Rambusch; a number of canopy and altar schemes were explored before the bronze baldachino was chosen. Other marble railings throughout the church were similarly replaced with bronze railing, harmonizing with the new baldachino. From the white marble predella, four bronze columns sweep upward to form a canopy over the altar, echoing the dome soaring high above. The form of the baldachino was adopted to heighten the experience of the interior by framing the high-relief panels in the four altars when viewed from any vantage point in the church. The other schemes considered for the canopy, while striking in their own way, would not have achieved such a dramatic viewing experience.

Every surface of the baldachino is covered with sculpted and enameled decoration. On the inner face of the columns stand bronze statues of the apostles with their views

Rambusch Brothers, Dome of the Baldachin in Memorial Church.

directed toward the altar. At the summit of each arch, where two columns meet, is the symbol of one of the Evangelists, and threading around the columns are running relief bands of ornamental floral designs and studies of birds of America, celebrating St. Francis' love of nature. In the ceiling of the baldachino is a brilliant enamel representation of Mary, Mediatrix of all Graces, offering prayers to the Holy Trinity for the salvation of humankind. Around this central motif is the Ave Maria in words and symbols. Medallions at the pendentives symbolize the Annunciation, the Visitation, the Birth of Christ, and the Assumption of the Virgin Mary, surrounded by the nine choirs of angels. Surmounting the baldachino—at the height of approximately thirty-five feet—is a bronze cross that continues the progression of the eye from the sparkling baldachino to the splendid dome that soars above.

To emphasize the upward vista toward the dome, four mural paintings depict the four Marys of the Gospels. These were painted by Mary Schiel in 1949 and installed in the dome's pendentives in 1950. It is believed that the four Marys of the Gospels would have gone to the tomb to prepare Jesus' body for burial according to Jewish custom. The oils and spices represented in these mural paintings would have been used for that purpose. Facing the Crucifixion Altar, the mural on the right depicts Mary Magdalene with St. John the Apostle and St. Peter and Mary at the Tomb. The mural on the left is the Virgin Mary with the instruments of the passion: the crown of thorns, the nails, and the spear. In her hands she carries the shroud to wrap the body of Jesus. Facing the Transfiguration Altar, the mural on the right is Mary the mother of James and John with an eagle; the eagle is the symbol of St. John the Evangelist. In Mary's hands are an incense lantern and a container of anointing oil. The mural on the left depicts Mary, the wife of Clopas, who holds in her hands a cloth with spices. Mary stands in a garden, and to her right is a tree that symbolizes the tree of knowledge in the Garden of Eden. On her left are three crosses representing the crosses of Calvary, the larger of which symbolizes Christ's cross.

The jubilee renovations transformed the interior of Memorial Church into the impressive Byzantine space that it remains to this day. The original interior was beautiful in its austerity, and the church as we see it now is equally beautiful with its reflected

Mary Schiel, *Mary, Wife of Clopas*, ca. 1949.

light and dazzling color. Fifty years since Friar Baumann's renovations, the church still sparkles and the color and light still affect our senses, but problems with parts of the aging church have begun to place it in serious jeopardy. In 2006 renovations to the dome and the ceiling of the vaults were begun to strengthen the church's overall structure, and to restore portions of the paint that had been damaged by water and the effects of age. When these renovations are complete, the interior will be as splendid as it was in 1899 and 1953, and for the next fifty years.

TOUR OF
THE MEMORIAL CHURCH

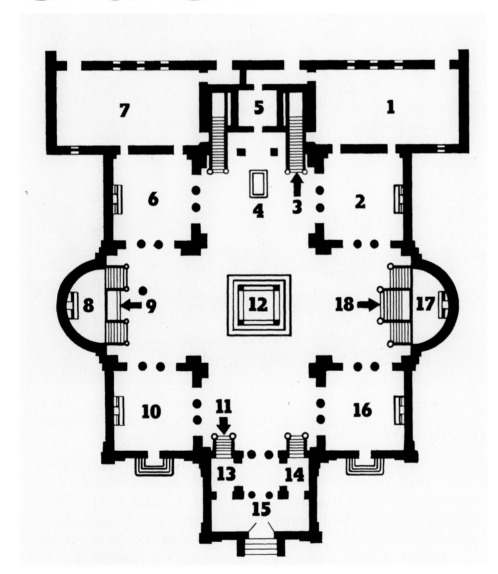

THE MEMORIAL CHURCH
 1. Lobby
 2. Chapel of St. Joseph
 3. Altar of Thabor
 4. Stone of Anointing
 5. The Holy Sepulcher
 6. Chapel of St. Francis
 7. The Blessed Sacrament Chapel
 8. Altar of the Holy Spirit
 9. Exit from the Grotto of Bethlehem
10. Lady Chapel
11. To the Altar of Calvary
12. Center Altar
13. Main Entrance
14. Chapel of St. Anthony
15. Sacred Heart Altar
16. Entrance to the Grottos

THIS TOUR OF THE MEMORIAL CHURCH MOVES IN A COUNTER-CLOCKWISE DIRECTION, BEGINNING WITH THE ENTRANCE FROM THE TOUR LOBBY INTO THE CHAPEL OF ST. JOSEPH.

Chapel of St. Joseph.

EASTERN WALL AND NAVE

Chapel of St. Joseph. The Chapel of St. Joseph, installed in 1909, was the final chapel to be completed in the church. The chapel, with its altar and the bas-relief panels above it, is very similar to how it looked at installation, although the bas-relief panels were painted around 1925-1927. While the other chapels contain work by James Earley, the father of John Earley, the stucco panels in this chapel were instead designed and executed by an unknown Danish sculptor who had studied in Düsseldorf and was a frequent visitor to the studio of the Franciscan sculptor Friar Hugo Linderath, located in the Düsseldorf Franciscan Friary. How the Danish sculptor received the commission for the altar reliefs is unknown. The panels represent the Wedding of Joseph and Mary, on the left, and the Flight into Egypt, on the right. The sculpted wooden panel and altar, located just inside the entrance, were installed in 1953. The wooden panel is from Italy, but the sculptor is unknown.

Altar of Tabor.

Gustav Doré, "The
Transfiguration,"
from *The Doré Bible
Illustrations* (New York:
Dover Publications,
1974).

Royal Bavarian Art Institute, *Trinity.*

Altar of Tabor and the Transfiguration. The Altar of Tabor was the first of the altars in the Memorial Church to be completed, and was installed in 1916. The large single relief panel, which depicts the moment of Christ's ascension into heaven, was based on the 19th century French artist Gustave Doré's concept of the Transfiguration from Mark 9: 1-8. The relief was sculpted in gypsum by artists working in Earley Studio and probably served as the model for the other three altars. There are three windows above the altar, a Trinity window, which was a gift of Cincinnati and New Orleans friends of the Monastery. The windows were designed by the Royal Bavarian Art Institute in Munich and installed in 1907, twenty years before the rest of the altar was completed. The central window panel represents God the Father with the Holy Spirit in a form of a dove at His feet. In the window on the left is depicted the Crusader's Cross, which was the emblem of the Crusader Kingdom of Jerusalem.

Conrad Schmitt Studios, Crusader Windows at the Altar of Tabor. *Knights Worshipping at the Holy Sepulcher, St. Francis before the Sultan*, and *The Death of a Crusader.* Below, *The Crusader's Vow, Mary Queen of Palestine, and The Blessing of a Crusader.*

The Crusader's Cross is composed of five separate crosses that represent the Body of Christ (central cross) and the wounds of the crucified body. The window on the right represents the Coat of Arms of the Franciscan Order.

Another group of stained-glass windows, depicting Crusaders, was installed on either side of the Altar in 1941. Designed by Conrad Schmitt Studios in Milwaukee, Wisconsin, the six windows are stripped of extraneous ornament in a return to a simplicity reminiscent of medieval stained-glass design. There are no borders and no effort to maintain symmetry of design, an effect that places them in contrast with the other pictorial windows in the church. The extreme austerity of the

Schmitt Studios' design, which the *Crusader's Almanac* called "Franciscan Simplicity," may also have been dictated by necessity since they were conceived at a time when the nation was just beginning to recover from the Great Depression and donations to the Monastery were less generous than previously.

The Crusader windows also differ from the rest of the stained-glass in the Memorial Church in that they do not receive natural light; instead, artificial light is transmitted from the Monastery Library and Cloister Choir, located on either side of the Altar of Tabor. To accommodate the lack of natural light, soft neutral tones were chosen for the window colors: topaz, rose, and a cloudy green, and the figures are distinguished from the ground only by black angular lines regularly interrupted by the lead panes. The windows to the right of the altar represent: *The Crusader's Vow*, *Mary Queen of Palestine*, *The Blessing of a Crusader*; the windows to the left of are: *Knights Worshipping at the Holy Sepulcher*, *St. Francis before the Sultan*, and *The Death of a Crusader*.

Beneath the Altar of the Transfiguration is a replica of the Holy Sepulcher in Jerusalem. According to ancient custom, the tomb was built with an antechamber or mourners' room, which is now known as the Chapel of the Angel. The Holy Sepulcher was one of the holy sites and shrines that architect Aristide Leonori measured and drew during his 1898 trip to the Holy Land, which ensured the exact reproduction of both the antechamber and tomb in the Memorial Church. The stucco reliefs covered in silver and bronze, which decorate the exterior and interior chambers of the Sepulcher, are by James Earley.

The fourteen Stations of the Cross also begin and end here, with Station I, *Jesus is Condemned,* on the north wall near the Chapel of St. Francis, and Station XIV, *Jesus is Laid in the Sepulcher,* on the south wall, near the Chapel of St. Joseph.

James Earley, *The Resurrection*, bas-relief sculpture in gypsum, ca. 1900.

NORTH WALL AND APSE

Chapel of St. Francis. The *Crusader's Almanac* for Winter 1907 celebrated the completion of the St. Francis altar, proclaiming, "The new altar of St. Francis is a grand monument erected by the generosity of our many friends and benefactors throughout the States. The Lady members of the Third Order at Mt. St. Sepulcher have also shown their love to St. Francis, by contributing generously to this noble piece of art." As a chapel for the founding saint of the Monastery's order, the installation of the Chapel of St. Francis and its altar was indeed cause for celebration.

James Earley designed the marble altar and the gypsum relief panels flanking the statue of St. Francis. The relief panel to the right depicts the St. Francis blessing St. Louis IX King of France and St. Elizabeth Queen of Hungary—royal members of the

Third Order who are also represented in stained-glass windows over the Holy Spirit Altar. To the left, St. Francis receives the stigmata of the five wounds of Christ. Louis IX (1214-1270) was the Crusader King of France who brought back from Jerusalem the crown of thorns, for which he built the Sainte-Chapelle in Paris; Sainte-Chapelle was subsequently destroyed during the French Revolution, although restored in 1837, and the crown of thorns is presumed to have been lost. Queen Elizabeth of Hungary (1207-1231) was known for her work among the poor and sick. Notable in a photograph from the 1930s is the wooden sculpture depicting St. Francis and Jesus at Calvary; this statue was replaced, probably during the, jubilee renovations, with the wooden sculpture that we see today of St. Francis holding a dove in his left hand. At this time, the Chapel of St. Francis was given a decorative ceiling frieze in tones of terra cotta, grey and green, depicting doves and fishes.

ST. FRANCIS AND JESUS AT CALVARY
Notable in a photograph from the 1930s is the wooden sculpture depicting St. Francis and Jesus at Calvary; this statue was replaced, probably during the, jubilee renovations, with the wooden sculpture that we see today of St. Francis holding a dove in his left hand.

Blessed Sacrament Chapel after renovations.

Altar of the Holy Spirit.

The Blessed Sacrament Chapel. The Blessed Sacrament Chapel was originally known as the Penance Chapel. The chapel was renovated in 1958 under the direction of Friar Baumann and Father Paschal Kinsel. The altar, by Rambusch Company, was installed at that time. The icons in this chapel are attributed to Russian Orthodox nuns of the convent at Mount of Olives in Jerusalem. The Stations of the Cross, designed in a contemporary Byzantine style, are also by Rambusch Company.

The Altar of the Holy Spirit. The Altar of the Holy Spirit is located in the apse across from the Altar of the Sacred Heart and next to the Chapel of St. Francis. A wooden altar was used here until 1925, when it was replaced by John Earley's design, made of Botticino marble and executed in Italy. The new altar was a gift of a benefactor who had earlier donated the replica of the Stone of Anointing. Surrounding the altar is a large relief panel designed by John Earley and sculpted by artists in his studio. The relief consists of three separate panels, each depicting scenes related to the Holy Spirit. The central panel depicts the Holy Spirit as a dove surrounded by angels and rays of celestial glory. The panel on the left depicts Christ commanding his disciples to go forth and preach the Gospel, and on the right, St. Francis of Assisi is shown sending his followers on missions of mercy and evangelization. Like the Altar of the Sacred Heart, the Altar of the Holy Spirit has nine windows. Windows one, five, and nine contain ornamental designs; window five contains a large emblem of the Holy Spirit, and windows one and nine contain emblems of the cross and book and the chalice. From left to right, the remaining six windows depict: St. Yves of the Secular Franciscan Order; St. Louis, bishop of Toulouse; St. Bonaventure; St. Elizabeth, Queen, of the Secular Franciscan Order; St. Agnes of Assisi of the Second Order; and St. Rose Viterbo of the Secular Franciscan Order.

Royal Bavarian Art Institute, windows for the Altar of the Holy Spirit.

Ludwig Könnel, *Panorama of Bethlehem*, ca. 1900-1910.

The Lady Chapel, ca. 1900.

Below the altar is the entrance to the Grotto of Bethlehem and the Catacombs. At the foot of the staircase is a panorama of Bethlehem, painted in the early 20th century by a German artist named Ludwig Könnel, about whom little is known. The Stations of the Cross continue here in the north apse, with Stations II through V: *Jesus Falls for the First Time*, *Jesus Meets His Holy Mother*, *Jesus Carries the Cross*, and *Simon Helps Jesus Carry the Cross*.

WEST WALL AND NAVE

The Lady Chapel. The first photographs of the Lady Chapel (originally known as the Altar of the Jubilee of the Immaculate Conception), taken around 1900, reveal just how much the chapel has evolved over the years. In 1900, the chapel consisted of a simple marble altar topped by a statue of the Virgin Mary. Like the rest of the church, the decoration was simple, with a light-colored paint and white trim. In 1906, James Earley designed the altar and the relief panels that make up the chapel as we see it today, with a few exceptions. The statue of Mary that appears in the photograph from 1900 remained at the altar at least until the 1930s. Today, however, she is replaced by a newer figure with an attached halo, painted in blue and white, the traditional colors of Mary's robe. The panel to the left represents the Presentation of Mary in the Temple, and the panel on the right, her Coronation in Heaven. During the jubilee renovations of the church painted decorations were added to the chapel ceiling. As seen today, the frieze, in muted tones of blue, grey, and terra cotta, has a stylized design that suggests common motifs, the moon and the globe, associated with Mary.

The eight stained-glass windows in the Lady Chapel were installed in 1931. From left to right, the four windows above the altar represent: St. Ferdinand V, King, of the Secular Franciscan Order, St.

Royal Bavarian Art Institute, windows for the Lady Chapel, with the windows over the altar in top photo.

Joachim, St. Anne, and St. Isabella, Queen, of the Secular Franciscan Order. Saints Anne and Joachim were the parents of Mary; Isabella and Ferdinand of Spain provided funds for the Crusades. The windows over the door depict, left to right: St. Hyacintha of the Secular Franciscan Order, St. Peter Baptist, Blessed John Duns Scotus, and St. Peter Alacantra; the Duns Scotus window may have been a replacement window installed at a later date, as the original order was for a window depicting St. Bede the Venerable.

The Altar of Calvary. According to reports published in the *Crusader's Almanac*, winter 1925, the marble altar, designed by John Earley, is an exact copy of the one that now stands over the crucifixion site on Calvary in Jerusalem. Earley included in his design an opening in the marble to replicate fissures caused in the rock by the earthquake that occurred at the time of Christ's death. Earley also designed the vast, life-size relief panel that spans the entire end of the nave, sculpted by artists working in his studio. The panel to the left depicts Mary, the Disciples, and the Good Thief, while the panel to the right depicts Christ's enemies overshadowed by approaching darkness; Mary Magdalene kneels at the base of the cross.

The triple stained-glass window above the altar and relief panel was, like the other windows in the church, designed by the Royal Bavarian Art Institute in Munich and installed in 1931. The central panel depicts St. Francis surmounted by the Coat of Arms of the Holy Land Franciscans, while to the left is St. Louis the King Crusader, and on the right is St. Helena, the mother of Emperor Constantine and benefactor of the Church of the Holy Sepulcher in Jerusalem;

the design for the window depicting St. Louis is loosely based upon Gustave Doré's illustration, "St. Louis at Jerusalem," from Alfred Trumble's *Sword and Scimetar: The Romance of the Crusades* (1886). As the Altar of Calvary faces west, the window designers used stippled glass to subdue the natural light as it filtered through the glass in the late afternoon and at sunset.

In 1916 Aristide Leonori donated the bishop's cathedra, or chair, placed near the entrance to the Lady Chapel. The cathedra is made of marble and inlaid with mosaic tiles and is surrounded by an intricate mosaic pattern laid into the church floor—all that survives of the original terrazzo marble floor. Across from the cathedra is the painting *Lady of Palestine* by Charles Bosseron Chambers, completed and installed in 1941. The Stations of the Cross are continued in the west nave with Stations VI through IX: *Veronica Wipes the Face of Jesus, Jesus Falls for the Second Time, Jesus Speaks to the Holy Women,* and *Jesus Falls for the Third Time.*

Gustav Doré, "St. Louis at Jerusalem."

SOUTH WALL AND APSE

The Chapel of St. Anthony. The Chapel of St. Anthony of Padua (1195-1231) was installed between 1906 and 1909. The Chapel of St. Anthony has an altar and relief panels sculpted in gypsum by James Earley. The panels as installed were unpainted, as can be seen in a photograph of one of the panels in James Earley's studio. St. Anthony was originally an Augustinian who became a Franciscan after seeing the bodies of the first Franciscan martyrs brought back to Portugal from Morocco. St. Anthony was revered as a miracle worker and healer of the sick, as represented in the panel on the left, and a staunch friend of the poor, to whom he is shown ministering in the panel on the right.

James Earley, panel of the Chapel of St. Anthony, ca. 1906.

Royal Bavarian Art Institute, windows for the Chapel of St. Anthony. The windows above the altar are in the top photograph.

The stained-glass windows were installed in 1931. Over the altar are represented four Saints of the Secular Franciscan Order, from left to right: St. Elzear, St. Delphina, St. Roch, and St. Coletta. St. Roch was the son of a wealthy merchant who gave up his wealth to live among and care for the poor and sick. St. Delphina and her husband, St. Elzear, were royal patrons of the Franciscans. St. Colette founded the Colettine Poor Clares in 1381. The emblem just below the feet of the saints is the Crusader's Cross. The other four windows depict, left to right: St. Francis Solanus, St. Godfrey, St. Leonard of Port Maurice, and St. Mary Frances of the Third Order.

Royal Bavarian Art Institute, windows for the Altar of the Sacred Heart (composite photograph).

The Altar of the Sacred Heart. The Altar of the Sacred Heart is located in the south apse, next to the Chapel of St. Joseph and directly across from the Altar of the Holy Spirit. The altar itself is made of Italian marble, designed by John Earley and executed by McBride Studios. The three-panel bas-relief in life-size was designed by Earley and installed in 1925. It consists of three separate narratives from the life of Christ and St. Francis. The central panel depicts Christ enthroned as the "King and Center of All Hearts" and adored by Saints Francis and Clare of Assisi. The panel on the left represents Christ appearing to the Disciples when his wounds are revealed to "doubting" Thomas. On the right panel, a nobleman who was incredulous of St. Francis' stigmata now views them on the saint's corpse, and then kneels with other followers of St. Francis.

Above the altar are nine stained-glass windows by the Royal Bavarian Art Institute, installed in 1931. The central window contains an ornamental emblem with the Holy Land depicted in the center; the two outer windows also contain emblems of the lamb and the pelican. Both the lamb and the pelican are symbols of Christ the Redeemer. While the lamb is a commonly known symbol, the pelican was thought to feed its young with its own blood, making it a similarly appropriate emblem for Christ. The other six windows depict, from left to right, St. Bernardine, St. John Capistran, St. Paschal, St. Clare of the Second Order, St. Margaret Mary (to whom the Sacred Heart appeared), and St. Veronica Juliani of the Secular Franciscan Order.

Charles Svendsen, *Youth in the Temple,* before 1914.

Beneath the altar is a staircase leading to the Grotto of Nazareth and the Catacombs. Above the staircase is an oil painting, *Youth in the Temple,* attributed to the artist Charles Svendsen, and painted before 1914. The Stations located in the southern apse depict the final moments before the crucifixion and the death of Jesus, Stations X through XIII: *Jesus is Stripped of His Garments, Jesus is Nailed to the Cross, Jesus Dies on the Cross,* and *Jesus is Taken Down from the Cross.* The final Station, Station XIV, *Jesus is Laid in the Sepulcher* is located in the East Nave.

THE GROTTOS AND CATACOMBS

The grottos and catacombs were constructed at the same time as the Memorial Church, although some modifications have been made over time. It was much more difficult to visit Europe and the Holy Land at the beginning of the twentieth century than it is today, and the grottos and catacombs were designed to provide pilgrims with copies of these shrines and sites in lieu of an on-site visit. During his trip abroad in 1898, Aristide Leonori measured many of the sites, and he, James Earley, and John Earley later used these plans, as well as photographs, to reconstruct the shrines at the Monastery. The Earleys used stucco to give the walls of the catacombs and crypts a rock-like appearance, and countless unknown artisans were employed to paint the walls with decorations similar to the original shrines. Elsewhere, cement and stucco walls were painted to look like marble or stone blocks, an appearance that in some instances is remarkably life-like.

TOUR OF THE
CATACOMBS & CRYPTS

THE TOUR BEGINS AT THE ENTRANCE TO THE GROTTO OF NAZARETH, LOCATED BENEATH THE ALTAR OF SACRED HEART, AND MOVES THROUGH THE CATACOMBS INTO THE MARTYRS' CRYPTS AND THE PURGATORY CHAPEL AND EXITS THROUGH THE GROTTO OF BETHLEHEM, LOCATED BENEATH THE ALTAR OF THE HOLY GHOST.

Charles Svendsen (attr), *St. Anne with Mary* (left), and *St. Joseph Teaching Jesus* (right).

Grotto of Nazareth. Above the entrance to the Grotto of Nazareth is the painting *Jesus in the Temple*, painted by Charles Svendsen around 1907. At the bottom of the stairs are two altars to St. Joseph and St. Anne, over which are installed two paintings, also attributed to Charles Svendsen and executed around the same time. On the right, Joseph is depicted teaching Jesus, and on the left, St. Anne is similarly engaged with her daughter, Mary. Through the archway is an altar dedicated to the Annunciation, which is a replica of the shrine as it exists today in the Basilica of the Annunciation in Nazareth. John Earley designed the marble altar; the bas-relief behind it was

Left: John J. Earley and James Earley, Altar of the Annunciation in the Grotto of Nazareth. Right: Charles Bosseron Chambers (attr.), *St. Joseph and the Infant Jesus.*

designed by his father, James Earley; both were installed by 1907. The bas-relief, like the sculptural panels in the chapels in the Memorial Church were originally unpainted. The black marble column to the left of the altar replicates the column in the original shrine, which according to tradition, continued to hold up its roof even after being destroyed by looters. The doorway just beyond the Annunciation Altar leads to a small grotto that contains a very simple altar by John Earley and a painting of Joseph holding the Infant Jesus, attributed to Charles Bosseron Chambers. Both were installed in 1932, although the painting might have been created at an earlier date.

Altar of St. Benignus. St Benignus, a Roman general, was a 2nd century martyr put to death under the Roman Emperor Marcus Aurelius. Under the altar is a modern reproduction of a Renaissance sculpture of the saint. In his hand he holds a palm frond, which signifies his status as a martyr for the faith. The fresco-like paintings surrounding the altar were done by Charles Svendsen after the ancient style of the Catacombs. Behind the altar is depicted Jesus with His hand raised in blessing. The inscriptions are in Greek, which was the language of the church until after the 2nd century, when Latin came into more common use. The Alpha and Omega (A and Ω) are the first and last letters of the Greek alphabet, and in Christian iconography represent Jesus, the beginning and the end. The Chi and Rho (X and P) also symbolize Christ. The tablet, inscribed ZHCEC, meaning, "Thou shalt live," symbolizes steadfast faith. Delta (Δ) represents the Trinity. Other symbols in the painting also have meaning in Christian iconography. The Phoenix symbolizes the Resurrection of the body; the tree bearing fruit, sheltering a lamb, is a symbol of the church; the serpent with an inscription, which translated means, "In this sign you will conquer," represents Christ conquering evil; the fish, or dolphin, is another ancient symbol of Christ, as is the lamb, depicted here standing on a rock from which four rivers, depicting the four Evangelists, flow. The two mural paintings across from the altar are also by Charles Svendsen, and depict St. Benignus and St. Stephen, the church's first martyr, who was stoned to death.

Altar of St. Benignus.

Charles Svendsen, *St. Stephen* (left) and *St. Benignus*.

The Purgatory Chapel today.

The Purgatory Chapel. An early photograph of the Purgatory Chapel, taken around 1900, reveals a space dramatically different from the chapel as it exists today. In 1931, the black Belgian marble altar, on a raised dais, was installed, and it is likely that the mural paintings, seen in this photograph from that time, were also placed on its walls. During the jubilee renovations, the Purgatory Chapel was again redecorated. A polychromed, wooden bas-relief panel from France, depicting the Virgin Mary and Angels ministering to souls in Purgatory, was installed beneath the altar; also at this time, the mural paintings were covered with mosaic work executed by local artists. The large mosaic to the right, "Ye dry bones, hear the word of the Lord," depicts a scene from Ezekiel 37:1-14. This vision is not of the

The Purgatory Chapel ca. 1900 (above) and 1931 (below).

resurrection of the body, but a representation of the revival of the nation of Israel, which had fallen into the worship of false gods. The graves depicted symbolize the Diaspora, or the Israelites inhabiting foreign lands. The other large mosaic, to the left, depicts Jesus' body being prepared for burial after being taken down from the cross by Joseph of Arimethea and Nicodemus. The other figures represent St. John, Mary, St. Mary Magdalene, and another Mary of the Gospels. The two mosaics on the walls flanking the exit from the chapel to the Martyrs' Crypts, "To Death" and "To Life," depict physical death and spiritual rebirth. The small mosaic to the right of the entrance to the Chapel is Jesus raising Lazarus from the dead.

Murals in the Martyrs' Crypt depict St. Thecla (left) and St. Venantius (right). The artist is unknown.

The Catacombs and Martyrs' Crypts. From the Purgatory Chapel a short passageway leads to the Catacombs and Martyrs' Crypts, which were constructed around 1915. The two stairways leading from this passage contain murals depicting scenes in the lives of two martyrs. The murals were painted by an unknown artist and probably installed during the jubilee renovations. The stairway on the left contains a scene from the story of St. Thecla of Iconium, a 1st century saint. After hearing St. Paul preach, Thecla took a vow of chastity, thwarting the wishes of her parents who had promised her in marriage—a legal contract which meant Thecla broke the law with her vow. For breaking the law and her conversion to Christianity, Thecla was ordered to be burnt at the stake, but a storm put out the fire; she was then sent to the amphitheatre to be devoured by beasts, which is the scene depicted here. Miraculously, the animals refused to attack her and she later joined St. Paul in Myra where she became known for other miracles. In the stairway on the right is a scene depicting the martyrdom of St. Venantius. According to legend, Venantius was only seventeen when he was tortured for his faith before being sent to the lions in the amphitheatre. Like St. Thecla, he was miraculously saved from the lions but was later beheaded.

Past these staircases is a small passageway that replicates the burial cavities, known as loculi, in the Catacombs in Rome. The walls of the cavities are decorated with ancient symbols and inscriptions in Latin. This passageway leads to the Grotto of Bethlehem. Continuing straight ahead is an antechamber decorated on all sides with frescoes similar to those found in the ancient Catacombs. Leading from this antechamber are chapels for two other martyrs, St. Cecilia, a Roman martyr of the 3rd century (top) and St. Sebastian, a Roman martyr of the 2nd century. St. Cecilia, like St. Thecla, was a young Christian who had taken a vow of chastity yet was engaged to a Roman named Valerian. She converted Valerian and he was later martyred. When Cecilia was brought before the Roman governor, she was sentenced to death by strangulation, which failed; Cecilia was then sentenced to be beheaded, but three blows failed to sever her head from her body. Because she was said to be a musician in life, St. Cecilia is the patron saint of musicians and in 1584 she became the patron saint of the Academy of Music in Rome. St. Sebastian was a captain of the Roman guard under the Emperor Diocletian. When it was discovered that he was a Christian, he was shot many times with arrows and later beaten to death. He is the patron saint of archers and soldiers.

The Martyrs' Crypts of St. Cecilia (top) and St. Sebastian (bottom).

James Earley, Nativity altar in the Grotto of Bethlehem, ca 1909, as it appeared in 1950.

Mosaic in the Nativity altar.

Charles Svendsen, *The Nativity* and *Adoration of the Magi*, before 1914.

The walls of both chapels are decorated with fresco-like paintings of scenes from the Old and New Testaments, probably painted by Charles Svendsen or by local artists under his direction. The Chapel of St. Cecilia contains a modern copy of a sculpture of the saint by the Renaissance master Maderno; the original is located in the Catacombs of St. Callistus in Rome. The Chapel of St. Sebastian also contains a reproduction of a Renaissance sculpture by Bernini. Bernini created many of the sculptures that decorate St. Peter's Basilica in Rome and also designed the basilica's famous colonnade. The marble sculptures were installed during the jubilee renovations, replacing plaster sculptures by Earley Studio.

The Grotto of Bethlehem. The Grotto of Bethlehem, or Nativity Grotto, is a copy of the original Cave of Nativity in Bethlehem, over which Queen Helena and her son, Emperor Constantine, erected a basilica in 315 A.D. Originally, a relief sculpture by James Earley was installed in the grotto above the Nativity altar, and a choir of angels, painted by Charles Svendsen, decorated the wall behind it. The mosaic that is above the altar today was installed in 1980, and is a copy of the original Byzantine mosaic in the Cave of Nativity in Bethlehem.

To the right of the altar is another grotto as well as a smaller altar that commemorates the visit of the Magi to Bethlehem. On two walls of the grotto is a diptych, *The Nativity and Adoration of the Magi*, attributed to Charles Svendsen and painted before 1914 in an early Renaissance style.

The exit from the grottos leads into the north apse, beneath the Altar of the Sacred Heart. The panorama, *City of Bethlehem*, installed in the wall of the stairway, was painted in the early 20th century by the artist Ludwig Könnel.

Detail, Rosary Portico, designed by Murphy & Olmsted and John J. Earley.

Monastery
Grounds & Gardens

T he Monastery grounds have a history that dates back, at least in written terms, 300 years to a Royal Patent granted by King Charles I to Cecil Calvert, 2nd Lord Baltimore, in 1632. The land was originally part of Somerset County, Maryland, established in 1666 by Lord Baltimore, which stretched from the Chesapeake Bay to the Atlantic Ocean, and from the Virginia line to the Nanticoke River. In 1688, a 500-acre tract of land referred to as Cuckold's Delight was surveyed for William Layton, a former indentured servant. How the tract received its humorous—and in hindsight, rather ironic—name has been lost over time, but another tract in the area was referred to as Trundle Bed Cuckold, demonstrating the early colonists' sense of humor! In any event, the tract containing the 100 acres that would eventually form the Monastery's property passed through several owners during the next 200 years, including Arthur Nelson, one of the largest land-owners in Prince George's County in the 1720s. By 1845 it was owned by

The Franciscan Monastery from the south, ca. 1900.

the Patterson family, and in 1861, Fort Bunker Hill was built on an adjacent piece of land. When the Monastery was under construction, workers found canon balls and bullets embedded in the dirt, a legacy of the property's proximity to a fort active during the Civil War. In 1869, the land was surveyed for Harriet McCeeney, who purchased the property that would later be sold to Father Godfrey Schilling in 1897.

Although Schilling had ambitious plans for developing the land to create replicas of sites and shrines in the Holy Land, from its inception, the Monastery was intended to be self-sustaining, and in addition to the orchard and vineyard, the friars maintained a kitchen garden, raised chickens and cattle, and farmed the meadow to the east. The now resplendent gardens surrounding the Friary and Memorial Church were much more humble at the turn of the century, and the lower gardens and

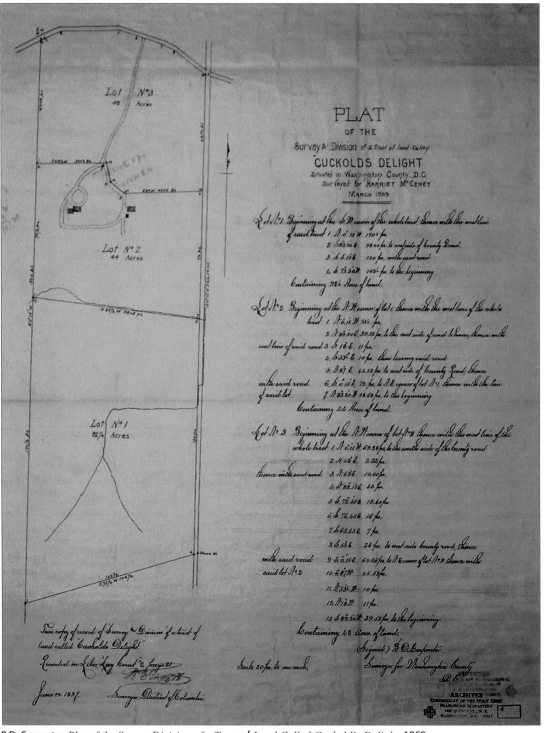

B.D. Carpenter, *Plat of the Survey Division of a Tract* of *Land Called Cuckold's Delight*, 1869.

Above: A friar farming the Monastery's fields, ca. 1900. Below: Plan of the Monastery grounds, ca. 1900.

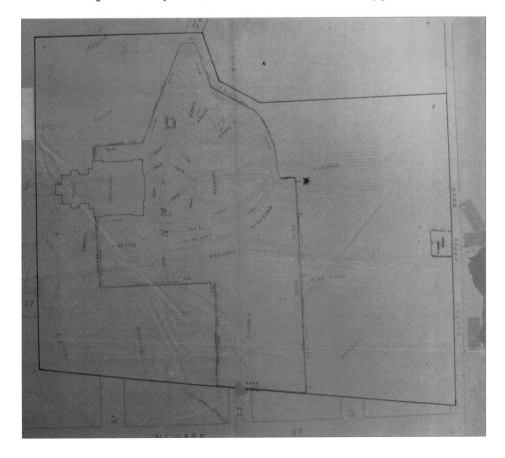

Above: Workmen clearing the side of the hill for the shrines and grottos. Below: The Grotto of Lourdes, ca. 1920.

grottos that cover the south hill of the Monastery site are located in an area that was originally intended to be an orchard and vineyard. However, in 1903, the Monastery began to clear much of the hill and the surrounding area for the grottos and shrines. The project, which included clearing the land and removing a large portion of the hill, took several years to complete. The first grotto, the Grotto of Lourdes, was completed in 1913, and the other shrines were completed during the subsequent decade. Both the upper gardens and lower gardens of the Monastery were originally overseen by Friar Meinrad Wiget (d. 1965), and until 1995, the friars did all the gardening themselves. Since then, the planning, design, and maintenance of the Monastery's gardens has been in the care of landscape professionals.

TOUR OF THE
GARDENS

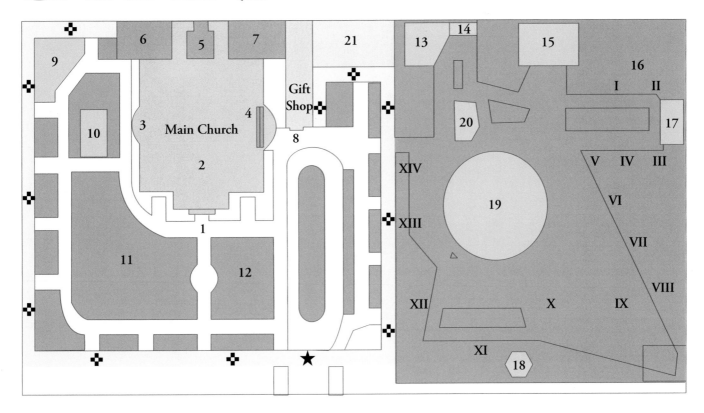

THIS TOUR STARTS IN THE UPPER GARDENS WITH THE ROSARY PORTICO BEGINNING AT THE FRIARY, MOVING AROUND THE PORTICO TO THE ORIENTAL GARDEN, ACROSS THE PIAZZA, AND THEN ENDS WITH THE GROTTOS.

LEGEND

★ Main Entrance
✠ Rosary Portico
1. Church Entry
2. Main Altar
3. Bethlehem
4. Catacombs
5. Tomb of Christ
6. Blessed Sacrament Chapel
7. Tour Lobby
8. Gift Shop Entry
9. Oriental Garden
10. Portiuncula
11. Friar-Priest Godfrey Schilling †1934
12. Saint Francis
13. Grotto of Gethsemane
14. Jewish Tomb
15. Tomb of Mary
16. The Stations of the Cross (I-XIV)
17. Saint Anne
18. Ascension Chapel
19. Lourdes Grotto
20. Lower Gardens
21. Friary

Murphy & Olmsted, The Rosary Portico (watercolor rendering of final design), 1918.

ROSARY PORTICO

The Rosary Portico, which encloses the Monastery and its upper gardens, originally developed from a need for greater safety and privacy. By 1918, the area surrounding the Monastery, known as Brookland, was becoming more densely populated, and increased traffic from pilgrims and other visitors motivated the friars to find a way to enclose the main entrance to the Monastery in a way that was practical as well as stylistically consistent with the architecture of the Memorial Church. The friars settled on a design submitted by architects Murphy & Olmsted, who were then designing buildings at Catholic University and were also involved at that time in the design and construction of the National Shrine of the Immaculate Conception. With Murphy & Olmsted's offices just down the hill from the Monastery, and the architects' experience constructing religious buildings using period styles, it was a perfect fit.

Murphy & Olmsted submitted a design in 1918 that was loosely based on the Cloister of St. John Lateran in Rome and the Church of Our Lady of St. Luke outside Bologna. A watercolor rendering from 1918 shows the Rosary Portico much as it looks today, but Murphy & Olmsted had also considered a circular as well as semi-circular plan.

Construction of the Rosary Portico, ca. 1925-1926.

In the Winter 1918 *Crusader's Almanac*, the friars called the proposed Rosary Portico the Monastery's "crown of glory." Lack of funding, however, delayed its immediate construction. To raise money, the Monastery circulated memorial cards for the "Arcade of the Saints" which tracked each five-cent contribution to the construction effort. By 1925 enough money had been raised to meet the $95,000 estimate submitted by John Earley to execute Murphy & Olmsted's design using the Earley Process. Although the Earley Process, as seen elsewhere in Washington, was celebrated for the mosaic-like colors and patterns Earley achieved in concrete, a neutral color was chosen for the Portico in order to harmonize with the yellow brickwork used for the church. The beauty of the Earley Process can be seen in the elegant turn of the columns covering Cloister Walk and in the façade decorations around the perimeter of the Portico, which is covered with emblems and symbols such as the lion, lamb, and pelican, and other designs consistent with Christian symbolism and early Romanesque architecture.

Four of the fifteen mosaic Mysteries of the Rosary located in the Cloister Walk.

Construction of the Portiuncula Chapel, 1925-1926.

The Rosary Portico, which covers 1,100 square feet, was completed and dedicated in 1926. There are fifteen chapels, corresponding to the fifteen mysteries of the Rosary, which contain mosaic panels and Ave Maria tablets. The chapels originally contained a bas-relief in the Earley Process but these were replaced in the early 1950s by the mosaic panels currently in place. The Ave Maria tablets, which bear the Angelic Greeting in nearly two hundred ancient and modern languages, were installed in the Rosary Portico in 1935. Designed by Murphy & Olmsted, the ceramic tiles were executed by Pewabic Pottery in Detroit, Michigan, a firm renowned for its Arts & Crafts tiles and pottery. There are two additional chapels that contain mosaics commemorating the Institution of the Secular Franciscan Order by St. Francis of Assisi in 1209-10 and the Blessed Virgin giving the Franciscan Crown to a friar. The mosaics in Cloister Walk begin with those dedicated to architect Aristide Leonori and Father Charles Vissani, to the right of the visitor entrance, and then proceed around the Portico to the other side of the gardens.

Right: Aristide Leonori, *Misure dell'ebtifigio'della Portiuncola*, ca. 1897. Below: C. Piati, *Rilevamento della Portiuncola*, ca. 1897-1909.

THE PORTIUNCULA CHAPEL (ST. MARY OF THE ANGELS)

The Portiuncula Chapel in the Monastery Gardens is a reproduction of a 4th century church, built on a tract of land less than a mile from Assisi, Italy. A gift of the Benedictine Order to St. Francis, the chapel was restored by the saint himself, and is venerated as the cradle and Mother Church of the Order.

The Portiuncula Chapel today.

The Monastery's reproduction of this chapel was constructed between 1925-1926. Like many other structures and shrines at the Monastery, it is based upon meticulous drawings and measurements, probably executed by Aristide Leonori or another Italian architect, C. Piato, around 1909-1915. These drawings, which still exist in the Monastery's archives, became the basis for architectural plans drawn by Murphy & Olmsted. Although the original drawings replicate the 14th century frescos, Murphy & Olmsted chose instead

The Portiuncula Chapel today.

After Hilarius of Viterbo, *Annunciation Altarpiece.*

to design the chapel in Potomac stone and to envision it as it might have appeared when first constructed and later restored by St. Francis. The Byzantine crucifix and altarpiece, the only decoration in the chapel, is a reproduction of Friar Hilarius of Viterbo's 1393 painting of the Annunciation, the altarpiece of the original Portiuncula Chapel. The marble altar was designed by John Earley.

THE UPPER GARDENS AND PIAZZA

There are three sculptures on the piazza in the upper gardens between the Portiuncula Chapel and the entrance to the lower gardens and grottos.

Friar Father Godfrey Schilling (d. 1934). This bronze sculpture is the work of Frederick C. Shrady, who also designed the mosaics decorating the vestibule entrance to Memorial Church. Cast in bronze in Milan in 1955, the sculpture depicts the Monastery's founder.

St. Francis and the Turtledoves. The statue of St. Francis and the Turtledoves is the work of sculptor Porfirio Rosignoli from Florence, Italy. Cast in bronze in Italy, it was installed in the piazza in 1916, a gift of the Secular Franciscan Order. Earley's base for the statue shows how color was used in the Earley Process to harmonize with the bronze of the sculpture.

St. Christopher. Greeting visitors at the front entrance to the Monastery and its gardens is Earley Studio's statue of St. Christopher, patron saint of travelers, completed around 1925 using the Earley Process.

Frederick C. Shrady, *Friar-Priest Godfrey Schilling*, 1955.

Porfirio Rosignoli, *St. Francis and the Turtledoves*, 1916.

John J. Earley and Earley Studio, *St. Christopher*, ca. 1925-1926.

THE LOWER GARDENS AND GROTTOS

Along the path through the gardens and valley are fourteen Stations of the Cross that were designed and built by the friars in 1916. Various other small shrines, such as that of St. Anthony of Padua, and mosaics, most of them erected during the 1960s and 1970s, are located throughout the garden walk.

The Grotto of Gethsemane. Completed in 1916, the Grotto of Gethsemane commemorates the garden in Jerusalem where Jesus suffered his agony. It is a replica of the original shrine on Mount of Olives in Jerusalem, which has been cared for by the Franciscans since 1392. John Earley supervised the construction of the grottos and other shrines, and he and the artists working in his studio designed many of their decorative elements. The Grotto of Gethsemane is constructed of reinforced concrete that was poured into a series of wooden molds to give it the shape of living rock. Inside the grotto is an altar and bas-relief panel of Jesus and an angel in the Garden of Gethsemane, both designed by Earley. Next to the grotto is a replica of a Jewish tomb at the time of Jesus, also constructed in 1916.

Above: The Grotto of Gethsemane under construction, ca. 1915. Below: Interior of the Grotto with the bas-relief panel by John J. Earley.

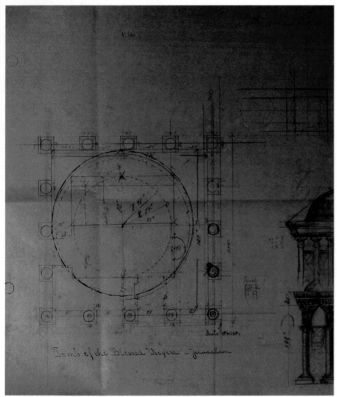 

Left: Aristide Leonori's measurements of the Tomb of the Blessed Virgin in Jerusalem. Right: The completed tomb.

The Tomb of the Blessed Virgin. During his visit to the Holy Land in 1898, Aristide Leonori completed a series of drawings of the Tomb of the Blessed Virgin in Jerusalem. These drawings served as the basis for the replica of that tomb in the Monastery's gardens, completed by John Earley in 1916 and dedicated on the Feast of the Assumption in August. The tomb is built as a mausoleum, with an outer structure enclosing an interior space, known as an edicule. Inside the tomb are a marble altar and a Byzantine-style painting of the Madonna and Child.

The Shrine of St. Anne and House of Cairo.

The Shrine of St. Anne and House of Cairo. The Shrine of St. Anne was also completed in 1916. The life-size sculpture of St. Anne, the mother of Mary, was donated to the Monastery by a benefactor who had visited the Shrine of St. Anne de Beaupré in Canada; the sculptor is unknown. The Shrine, housed in a cupola designed by John Earley, is situated above the replica of the house of Cairo, reputed to be the house occupied by Joseph, Mary, and the baby Jesus after their flight into Egypt. Similar to most of the shrines in the gardens, the House of Cairo was constructed by John Earley based on drawings and measurements brought back from the Holy Land by Aristide Leonori.

The Grotto of Lourdes under construction, ca. 1912.

The Grotto of Lourdes today.

The Grotto of Lourdes. The Grotto of Lourdes in the Monastery Gardens is an accurate copy of the original, a famous shrine in southern France where, in 1858, the Virgin appeared to a peasant girl, Bernadette, who was afterwards canonized. The Monastery's copy is based on drawings provided by a French architect in the late 19th century. Using these designs as a starting point, John Earley supervised the construction of the grotto, which began in 1912. Completed in August 1913, the grotto was dedicated on the feast day of the Assumption, and numerous dignitaries, including the Bishop of Matanzas, Cuba, attended the ceremony. Although constructed of poured concrete, Earley and his team took every effort to make the shrine look as though hewn from the living rock of Mt. St. Sepulcher. Over the years, the ivy growing over the Grotto has made this impression even more real.

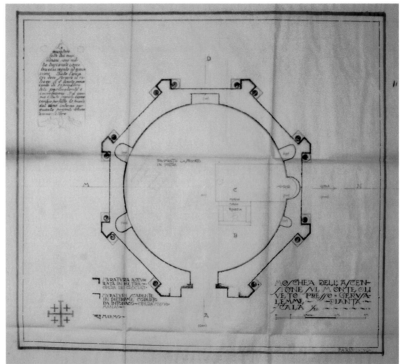

P. Ricci, *Pianta, Moschea dell'Ascensione sul Monte Oliveto Presso, Gerusalemme.*

The Chapel of Ascension.

The mosaics on the interior of the Chapel of Ascension dome by John J. Earley and Earley Studio.

The Chapel of Ascension. In June 1924, John Earley wrote to the Commissary, Father John Forest Donegan (d. 1959), that the Chapel of Ascension "will be an artistic reproduction of the Chapel of the Crusaders which was erected on the sight of the ascension (sic) on Mount of Olives near Jerusalem." Earley noted in his letter that, "although we approach this subject from an artistic and not an archeological point of view, nevertheless; I would like to make the structure as nearly authentic in form as is consistent with its environments." Earley did not design the chapel himself, instead he and his construction crew worked from measurements and plans drawn from the original on Mount of Olives at the turn of the century by an Italian architect, P. Ricci—making the Chapel of the Ascension as authentic a facsimile of the original as possible. The Chapel of the Ascension was completed in 1925 and blessed on the Ascension Day in 1926.

As with the Rosary Portico, then also under construction, Earley constructed the chapel in reinforced concrete using the Earley Process for both the interior and exterior surfaces. The color of the exterior surface was chosen to match the brickwork used for the Memorial Church and the Rosary Portico, but for the dome interior, which depicts the Ascension, Earley employed all the capabilities of his technique, and the results are magnificent. Earley had originally proposed covering the dome with mosaics "carried out in color and with materials similar to those employed in Venetian Mosaics." Although Earley employed the materials and colors of Venice, the implementation of the mosaic using the Earley Process represented an innovation of the traditional medium.

St. Francis Hall. Although not located within the gardens of the Monastery, St. Francis Hall represents the outer limits of the Monastery's grounds. Beginning in the 1920s the Monastery and its new shrines became the destination for thousands of pilgrims. Travel to the Holy Land itself was out of reach for most people, and pilgrims came from all over the United States and Canada, and some came from as far away as Central and South America. To meet the needs of these pilgrims, in 1930 the Monastery asked architects Murphy & Olmsted to design a building that would house necessary facilities such as a snack bar, restrooms, and a hall that could be used for dining, lectures, or services. The architects envisioned St. Francis Hall, then known as Pilgrimage Hall, in a variety of styles before settling on an austere Romanesque structure. St. Francis Hall was completed in 1931, and the first group to enjoy it that April was seventy-five pilgrims from the Catholic Young Women's Club of New York.

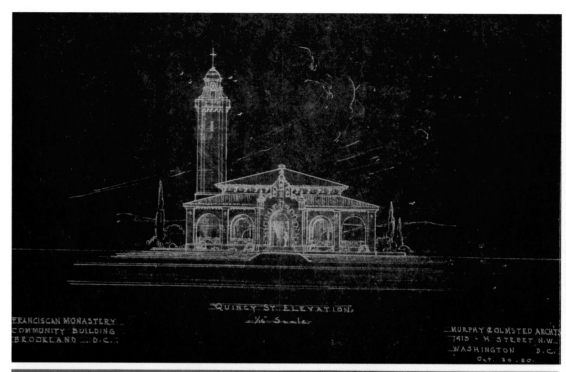

Murphy & Olmsted, designs for St. Francis Hall, 1930.

APPENDIX

PHOTOGRAPH CREDITS

Unless otherwise specified, all historic photographs belong to the Monastery Archives collections.

Monastery Archives
10, 11, 12, 13, 14, 15, 18, 20, 22, 26, 27, 29, 32, 33, 38, 39, 42, 43, 44, 55, 57, 58, 60, 75, 76, 80, 83, 84, 85, 86, 90, 91, 93, 94, 100, 101, 103, 104, 106

Brendan Cavanaugh
8, 30, 33, 38, 44, 46, 51, 52, 53, 56, 59, 60, 62, 63, 64, 66, 67, 68, 69, 71, 76, 77, 84, 92, 96, 97, 101, 104, 106

Michael Hoyt
16, 31, 80, 82, 87, 88
Kirsten M. Jensen
31, 32, 36, 37, 39, 40, 41, 55, 65, 64, 72, 73, 74, 78,

Owen Sweeney III
front and back cover, 28, 48, 51, 58, 74, 79, 95, 98, 99, 101, 102, 103, 104

page number	caption	photographer
cover 8	Cloister Walk	Owen Sweeney III Brendan Cavanaugh
10	Left: First Commissariat of the Holy Land in the United States, ca. 1890. Right: Front elevation, Commissariat of the Holy Land, architect unknown.	Monastery Archives
11	Father Godfrey Schilling and a companion at the pyramids in Egypt, 1907.	Monastery Archives
12	Above: The McCeeney House in 1897 Below: Early friars and neighbors on the hilltop where the Monastery now stands.	Monastery Archives
13	Above: Construction on the Memorial Church, ca. 1899. Below:The completed Memorial Church at the time of its dedication, September 1899.	Monastery Archives
14	Above: Dedication of the Monastery and its Memorial Church, Septemeber 17, 1899. Below: A view of the Monastery grounds and Brookland, ca. 1903.	Monastery Archives
15	Buses for pilgrims, parked along 14th Street, ca. 1930.	Monastery Archives
16	The Franciscan Memorial Church in springtime	Michael Hoyt
18	Aristides Leonori and Father Godfrey Schilling in the Monastery garden, ca. 1907-1909.	Monastery Archives
20	Leonori and Father Godfrey supervising the construction of St. Joseph's in Cairo, Egypt, 1909.	Monastery Archives
22	Earley Studio artisans scraping away the aggregate on the statue of St. Christopher, ca. 1926.	Monastery Archives
26	Murphy & Olmsted, Monastery Dome and Cupola Showing the proper silhouette, ca 1920.	Monastery Archives
27	Interior of the Memorial Church, ca. 1900, showing the Altar of Calvary and the Lady Chapel.	Monastery Archives
28	Interior of the Memorial Church.	Owen Sweeney III
29	Above: Murphy & Olmsted, Front Elevation, the Memorial Church, ca. 1920. Below, Hamilton & Wilson, Plan for Renovations to the Memorial Church and Friary, ca. 1940-1941.	Monastery Archives
30	Above: Frederick Shrady, "I am the Resurrection and the Life," mosaic, 1949, entrance to the Memorial Church. Below: Frederick Shrady, "Deus Meus et Omina," mosaic, 1949, entrance to the Blessed Sacrament Chapel.	Brendan Cavanaugh
31	Mosaics designed by Frederick Shrady in 1949 to decorate the exterior of the church vestibules.	Brendan Cavanaugh, Michael Hoyt, Kirsten M. Jensen
32	Above: Interior of the Memorial Church, ca. 1898, showing the Altar of Calvary and men laying the terrazzo floor.	Monastery Archives
32	Below	Kirsten M. Jensen
33	Murphy & Olmsted, Design for the Stations of the Cross, ca. 1933.	Monastery Archives, photograph by Brendan Cavanaugh
36	Royal Bavarian Art Institute, Christ Among the Doctors, The Sacred Heart, and The Institution of the Third Order.	Kirsten M. Jensen
37	Royal Bavarian Art Institute, Christ Giving the Keys to St. Peter, The Agony in the Garden, and The Resurrection.	Kirsten M. Jensen
38	Aristide Leonori, Front Elevation, Choir Loft (detail), ca. 1898.	Monastery Archives, photograph by Brendan Cavanaugh
39	Royal Bavarian Art Institute, Assumption of the Virgin (original conception, left), and Assumption of the Virgin window as installed in the Choir Loft.	Monastery Archives
	see above	Kirsten M. Jensen
40	Royal Bavarian Art Institute, Supper at Emmaus (left), St. Bonaventure (right).	Kirsten M. Jensen
	see above	Kirsten M. Jensen
41	Royal Bavarian Art Institute, St. Nicolas Tavelic(right) and St. Charles Boromeo (left).	Kirsten M. Jensen
	see above	Kirsten M. Jensen
42	Friar Cajetan Baumann and Rambusch Brothers, New color scheme for the Memorial Church, ca. 1949.	Monastery Archives
43	Friar Cajetan Baumann and Rambusch Brothers, Color Scheme for the Altar of Tabor, ca. 1949	Monastery Archives
44	Rambusch Brothers, two design conceptions for the new Main Altar.	Monastery Archives, photograph by Brendan Cavanaugh
45	Rambusch Brothers, dome of the Baldachin in Memorial Church.	Kirsten M. Jensen
46	Mary Schiel, Mary, Wife of Clopas, ca. 1949.	Brendan Cavanaugh
48	Interior of Memorial Church	Owen Sweeney III
49	Plan of Memorial Church]	
50	Chapel of St. Joseph.	Owen Sweeney III
51	Above: Altar of Tabor Below: Gustav Doré, "The Transfiguration," from The Doré Bible Illustrations (New York: Dover Publications, 1974).	Brendan Cavanaugh
52	Royal Bavarian Art Institute, Trinity.	Brendan Cavanaugh
53	Conrad Schmitt Studios, Crusader Windows at the Altar of Tabor. Above: The Crusader's Vow, Mary Queen of Palestine, and The Blessing of a Crusader. Below: Knights Worshipping at the Holy Sepulchre, St. Francis before the Sultan, and The Death of a Crusader.	Brendan Cavanaugh